AF327789

BALICH
SPECTACULAR
SHOWS

EDITED BY

LIDA CASTELLI AND MORENO GENTILI

Rizzoli
NEW YORK

New York · Paris · London · Milan

Marco Balich:
An Aesthetic of Emotions

Moreno Gentili

To introduce this book, in which we talk about great international ceremonies, we could begin by writing about the Olympics in ancient Greece, and of mythical athletes such as Pheidippides, the marathon runner from whom the Olympic legend was born, Acanthus of Sparta, Diagoras of Rhodes, and many more.

In fact, we will start from this, but from a quite different point of view. As protagonists of these pages, Marco Balich and his "dream team" hold a rightful place in the culture of the Olympics, thanks to their ability to inspire emotions by creating opening and closing ceremonies for the Olympic and Paralympic Games, or as creators of events celebrating countries all over the world.

These pages, then, will reveal skills that go beyond sporting ceremonies, encompassing prestigious events such as the Mexican Bicentennial, the Venice Carnival, shows on ice and on water, stadium openings for important football teams, and other similarly prominent happenings.

Visual, tactile, and auditory emotions, that are born out of a mix of imagination and technology made possible through the art of creative multitasking, are necessary to reach that sense of pleasure that connects form and content in any artistic act worthy of its name.

The work of Balich and of his group is wide-ranging, thanks to visions amplified by a very sophisticated technology as well as by a craftsmanship that is a reflection of an Italian style of design, which has gained recognition all over the world.

"Him I consider the architect, who by sure and wonderful reason and method knows both how to devise through his mind and energy, and to realize by construction, whatever can be most beautifully fitted out for the noble needs of man, by the movement of weights and the joining and massing of bodies," writes Leon Battista Alberti, architect, mathematician, musician, and philosopher from the 1400s and an exemplary representative of the innovative and boundless Humanism in which Balich believes.

Before going into an account of such an extensive creative production, let us delve for a moment into the history of the Olympics in Ancient Greece, which used to ratify a truce between populations at war and gave everyone the opportunity to compete on equal terms. We will do so from an unusual point of view, that of a brave woman named Callipateira. The mother of one of the athletes competing in Olympia, a place that women were forbidden to enter, she decided to contravene the law by disguising herself as a man, in order to train her son on the athletic field. She was discovered, but her deceit caused such a stir that the rules of the game were changed. From then on, athletes competed naked, complementing the concept of strength with a true "aesthetic of emotions," closer to the beauty of gods.

Callipateira, with her covert operation, tapped into the significance of the anthropological concept behind a beautiful *show*, and for this reason we are here today, representing what can be achieved by a ceremony, Olympic or institutional.

Let us now go back to the present time, to Marco Balich and his dream team, who, thanks to the seed planted by Callipateira, fused the concept of protocol with a kind of show that amazes the world with its universal themes delivered with extraordinary inventions never seen before.

Olympic ceremonies such as those of Torino 2006 and Sochi 2014, or celebrations such as the opening of the America's Cup World Series, are global events that highlight the exceptional qualities, applied to the creative production and technical engineering, of professionals working at the highest level in the world. Events of this scale, which leave no room for error, require months or years of organization to design complex sets, choreograph thousands of volunteers, study special effects, manufacture costumes, compose music, engineer scenic machinery, and much more.

It is a new understanding of show design that expresses itself in the form of a visual and technologically evolved narrative. The talent behind this creativity is based on a balanced relationship between a right measure of content and the effectiveness of a technology that is always at the forefront, capable of establishing a direct connection between the vision of the creators and the collective imagination of millions of people.

Marco Balich and his team possess the ability to transform a show into a visible and audible dream, and in fact to turn the *Impossible* into *I'm Possible*, as during Sochi 2014, when most of the world—even Ukraine, in the middle of a war crisis—stopped to watch the opening and closing ceremonies. A giant full-scale icebreaker forcefully entered the wide expanse of the stadium's field of play: a metaphor to illustrate how important it is to break down prejudices and to show bravery, for the future of humanity in serious need of peace, hope and prosperity.

The work of Marco Balich would not be so powerful if it did not enlist prestigious international artists for the construction of a *techne* so imbued with humanistic influences. To understand what the contribution of these people actually means, we should note that to manage a production of such magnitude, talent is not enough—social and cultural sensitivity is required. "The Olympics possess a unifying force stronger than the United Nations, as the whole planet feels a connection with the Olympic rings. This has meant that over the course of time the ceremonies of the Games have grown around a very strict protocol; attending these ceremonies has become the highest aspiration for the athletes of the whole world, and an unequaled peak in global TV audiences, with a presence of heads of state in numbers far superior to any other sporting or political event around the globe," claims Marco Balich with great conviction. These words hint at the possibility of establishing a model of relations between countries that is not based on the unfounded need for conflict, but on sharing values that are unifying rather than divisive.

The methodology described here is closer to that of a think tank, a framework usually linked to ideas and innovation. These types of show reveal truly astonishing scenic effects that stand as metaphors of high values, such as the massive wall built in the Torino 2006 Paralympic closing ceremony and torn down by a wheelchair, or the parade that filled the streets of Mexico City during the Bicentennial of Independence, which involved all of the country's indigenous ethnic groups.

The artistic choices of Marco Balich and his team are the result of intense discussion among the whole creative group and are a way of interpreting social reality

by staging a show that, according to the concept of "Feast," fills society's relational voids from an enlightened rather than obscurantist perspective. This concept has always embraced the necessity for a moment of relief and suspension from the burdens of daily life. With regards to the transformation of the "Feast in advanced modernity," the anthropologist Ernesto Di Renzo writes: "We begin to understand better the rituals of ancient times, the folk festivals, the Royal Entries, the urban festivities and their confraternities, the celebrations of a revolutionary frenzy. And we can count on descriptions and analyses of the rhythms and festive urges of very different cultures—from Bantu, Himba, or Ndembu rituals to the Rio Carnival, the Corpus Christi processions, the *Palio di Siena, Las Fallas* in Valencia or Thanksgiving in the United States."

The work that Balich performs in this sphere is brave and passionate; it overcomes the concept of show driven by consumerism and uninspired propaganda commonly held. Think of the parades imposed by dictatorships still capable of enforcing their autocratic vision of the world, or of the commercial events that are mere marketing tools. Parades and events, even when they are innovative, are very distant from the ceremonies and the values that they represent, and this is the substantial difference. The magical moments described in these pages are the opportunity for millions of people to experience a feeling of collective joy while taking part in a ritual that follows a strict protocol and alludes to profound themes.

"In the tea-room the fear of repetition is a constant presence. The various objects for the decoration of a room should be so selected that no color or design shall be repeated. If you have a living flower, a painting of flowers is not allowable. If you are using a round kettle, the water pitcher should be angular. A cup with a black glaze should not be associated with a tea-caddy of black lacquer," writes Kazuko Okakura in *The Book of Tea*.

It may sound easy to achieve, and maybe Balich and his dream team will reach perfection when they manage to put in practice what Okakura describes with painstaking precision. Those looking at the images in this book will notice how these ceremonies focus as much on the *detail* as on the *whole*—an approach capable of shortening the distance between small and huge, between a perfect tea ceremony and a moon landing, without reducing the emotions that these two experiences bring.

In conclusion, who is Marco Balich and how did he manage to emerge in the context of large-scale events? There are very few personalities who are able to reinvent the concept of "global show" and he undoubtedly belongs to this handful of creative minds.

Winner of an Emmy Award, Balich designed prestigious ceremonies such as those for UEFA Euro 2012, the Mediterranean Games in 2009, the inauguration of the Juventus and Shakhtar stadiums, the opening of the America's Cup World Series and many more. To this we should add the artistic direction of the Expo 2015 Italian Pavilion and the executive production of the Rio 2016 Olympic Ceremonies.

Hearing Marco Balich speak of his work is inspiring: "designing or producing Olympic Ceremonies is the most exhilarating and extraordinary human and professional adventure that my team and I could wish for in life."

His career began with international music, from which he learned the secrets behind the magic of a show. In the 1980s he worked to organize the concerts of Pink Floyd, U2, Peter Gabriel, and Eurythmics, while in the 1990s he produced several TV shows, managed TV channels such as Viva Television, and conceived the idea for the Heineken Jammin' Festival, Italy's biggest rock event. All this has resulted in a very eclectic professional background.

Balich combines different creative genres, as an architect does when mustering designers, engineers, workers and constructors to erect a large building into an organization in which nothing is left to chance, thanks to an exceptional creativity as well as impeccable management. "In this line of work you have to imagine a lot, and then be able to do very well what you have imagined," he says.

This kind of wide-ranging creativity is the result of a unique and exceptional thinking, translated into a visual language with three-dimensional dynamism. Unrepeatable emotions, that live and die in the moment.

We recall those "red skaters" shooting past us with a flame burning on their helmets during the Torino 2006 Olympics, a perfect example of how a moment of pure beauty can teach us a lot when it becomes an aesthetic of emotions. This is the recipe for shaping a creativity that is important not only aesthetically, but also content-wise. We are proud to consider this a part of the input that Italian design gives to the world.

We also remember the contribution that Balich and his team made in the context of the Paralympic Games. The strength of these experiences has made it possible to once again reduce the separation between able and disabled in a forward-thinking way.

"I believe that Paralympic athletes are equal to able-bodied ones, or actually even stronger. I love courage, people who challenge rules, who break the mold, and those who tear down barriers like the Paralympic athletes do, and as such are worthy of our admiration as much as the hundred-meter runner who breaks the nine-second barrier," claims Balich, echoing the words of Jean Baudrillard, who in his book *L'autre par lui-même* writes that "the disabled person is necessarily a potential expert in the motion and sensory field."

Now, image by image, the time has come to step into the magical world of visions that last only for the few moments in which they are staged. They are visions that have been in the collective imagination of the entire planet, and now here, on these pages, they definitely assert the absolute beauty of this new form of art, and reveal to an often amazed audience the inventiveness of a man who always transcends reality to reach his dreams.

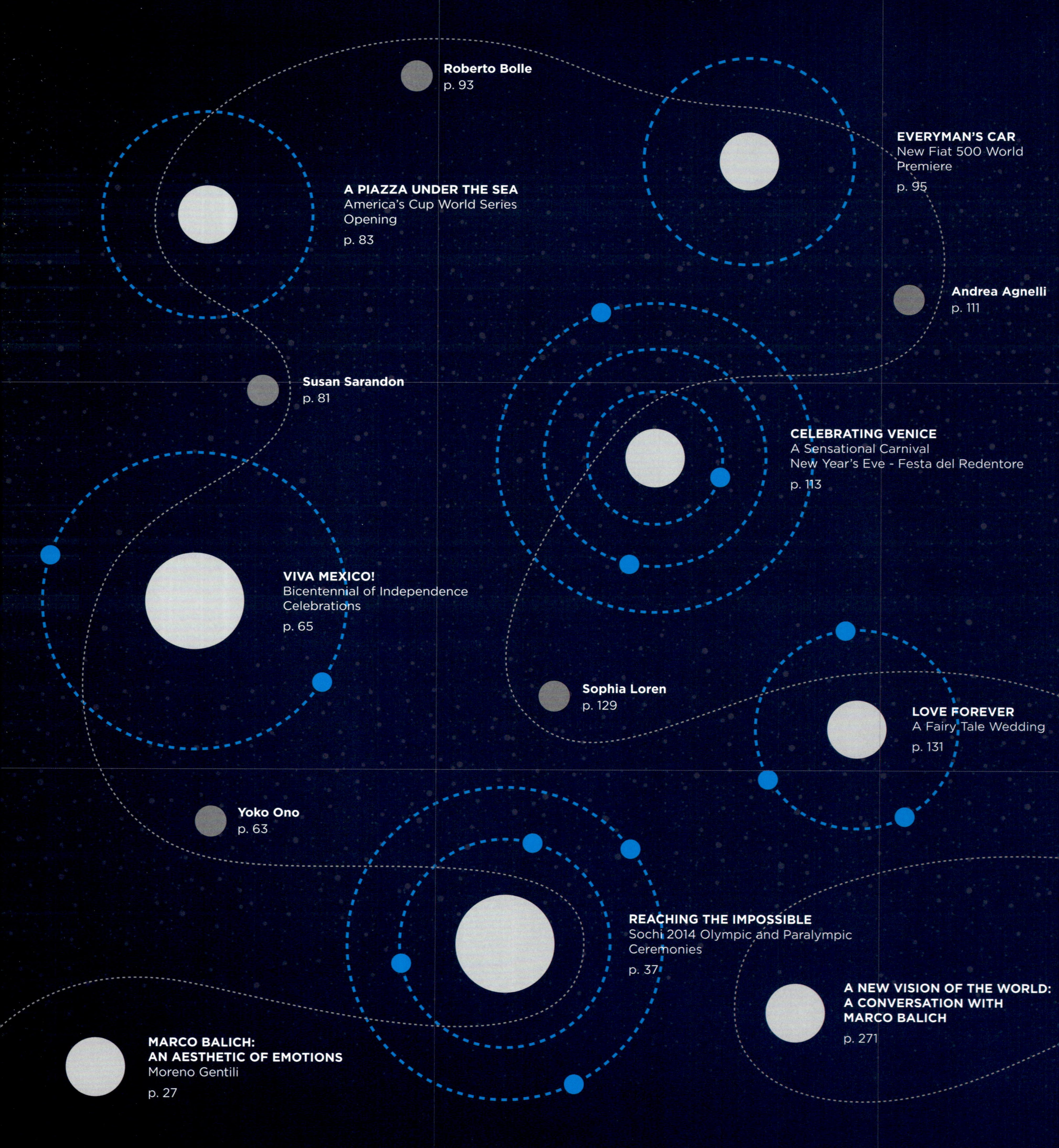

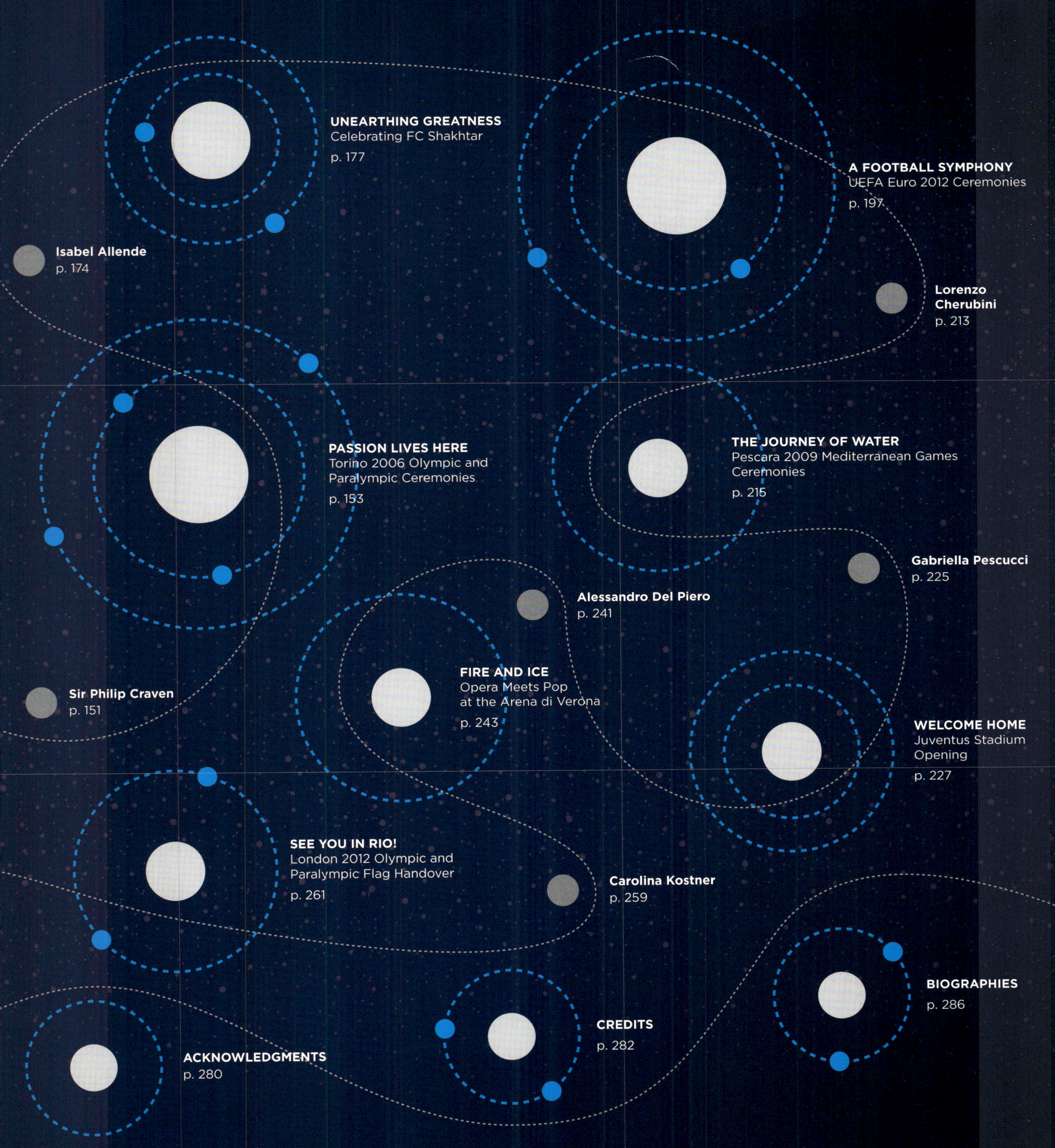

REACHING THE IMPOSSIBLE

Sochi 2014 Olympic and Paralympic Ceremonies

A sea that was as open and volatile as the destiny of human beings initiated the closing ceremony of the Sochi 2014 Olympics, ushering in a flying boat that symbolized the overcoming of adversity, as well as the aspirations and achievements, courage, and purpose connecting the millions of people watching from all over the world.

The sea moved, thanks to hundreds of volunteers dressed in silver costumes, creating patterns that gradually turned into the five Olympic rings minus one. The fifth ring, which during the opening ceremony failed to appear due to a technical fault, opened up after a few moments, demonstrating that even in international events of this scale it is fundamental to cultivate creativity and, when necessary, a fair measure of humor.

At this point the ceremony began with the entrance of the Russian flag in a sea of ice, which seemed to be dancing to the rhythm of those artistic and political movements of the twentieth century to which the Soviet Union made an extraordinary contribution.

The Sochi opening ceremony revealed an aesthetic in which set design and costumes expressed the poetic narrative of a continent: an upturned Chagall landscape moving above the heads of the audience; a multitude of pianos that invaded the field of play as a tribute to the Soviet music tradition; dance performances that paid homage to the legendary Bolshoi and Mariinsky, as a reminder of how dance has played a memorable part in the history of this land. And the story could not leave out theater, for which Chekhov represented a stylistic evolution with a unique emotional impact.

The intention of the Paralympic opening ceremony was to build a journey across yesterday's and today's Russia, its romantic transformation in a world rushing full steam ahead, toward a frenzied twentieth century aspiring to an unconditional modernity. The advance of an icebreaker was at the heart of one of the most dramatic scenes, as the ideal symbol of "ice breaking" among countries often caught in uncertain political situations, as the Ukrainian crisis of the time eloquently demonstrated.

The Paralympic closing ceremony, on the other hand, focused on a clear and poignant concept—*I'm possible*: in other words, nothing, or almost nothing, is impossible.

The three Sochi ceremonies were the result of a fruitful collaboration with a team of Russian producers. They ideally invited us to a necessary reflection on the future of nations, to believe that "impossible" is only an obstacle created in the wrong side of the field, that of the losers. The winners take risks and manage to overcome any challenge, be they able-bodied or with a disability. The vital energy of a man who lost his legs, climbing a rope up to the stadium's roof with the sole strength of his arms, stands as an emblem of these games and their deep significance—not as a mere demonstration of physical power, but as a representation of the indestructible and invincible will that human beings possess.

3) Герой отпускается из дома (В
часто исходит от самого героя,
благословение. Иногда герой не
просится погулять и пр., а на сам

...чаях инициатива отправки
...ителя. Родители дают
...их подлинных целей. О...
...на борьб...

АВАРИЙНЫЙ ВЫХОД
С1
С2

PO

SIGLE

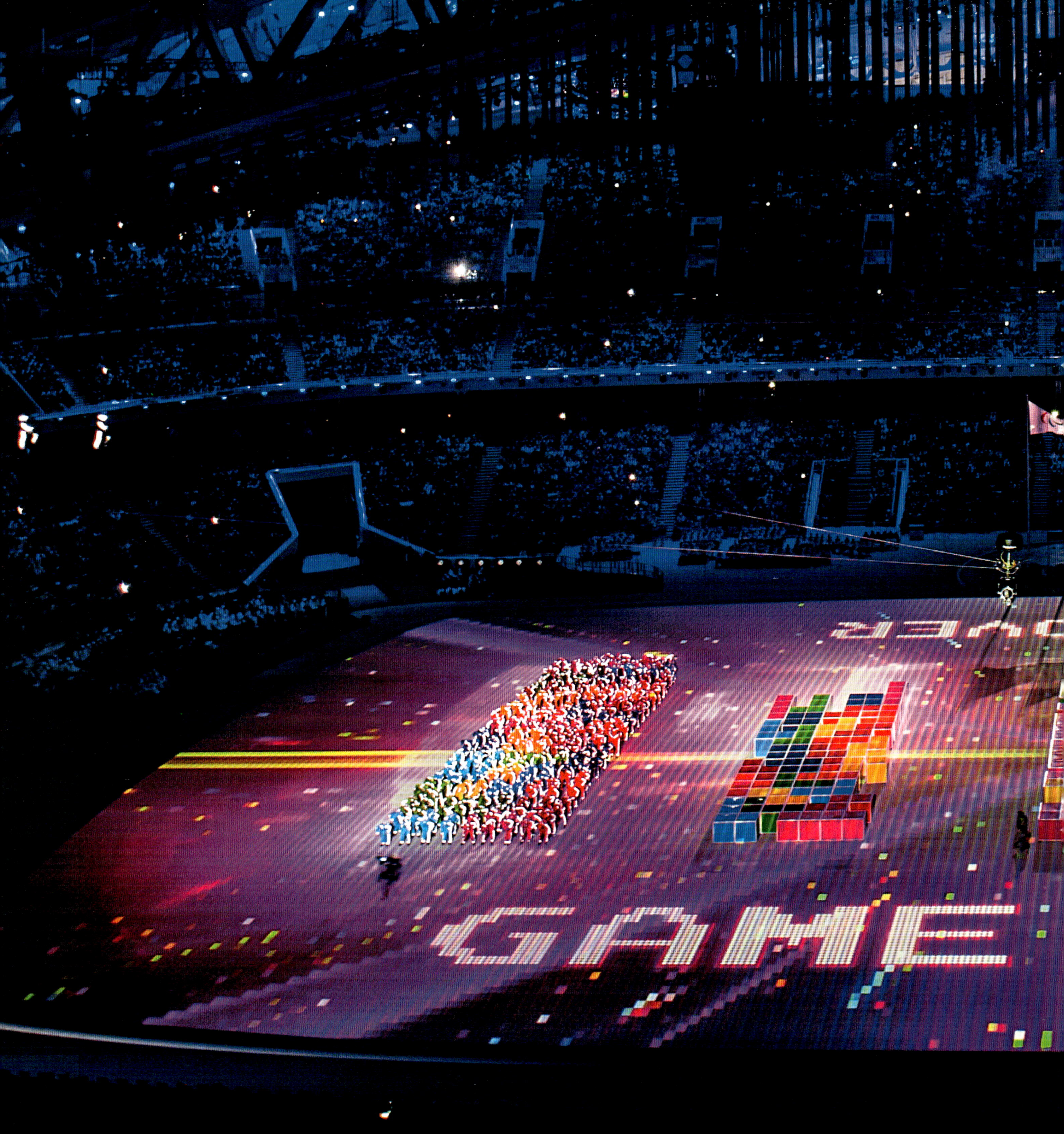
GAME

GAME
OVER

"Imagine Peace."

Imagine Peace.

You may think, how are we going to get one billion people to think peace?

Because if one billion people in the world think peace, we will get peace.

Remember each one of us has the power to change the world.

Power works in mysterious ways.

You don't have to do much.

Visualize the domino effect and just start thinking peace.

The message will circulate faster than you think.

It's time for action.

And the action is peace.

Spread the word.

Spread peace.

As my husband and partner, John Lennon, said,

"Imagine all the people living life in peace."

Yoko Ono

VIVA MEXICO!

Bicentennial of Independence Celebrations

An event celebrating the bicentennial of a country as complex as Mexico requires an all-encompassing creative project. A history of nobility and destitution, revolution and redemption are all feelings that define the Mexican people today, making them one of the most restless nations ever.
The Latin soul animating Mexico is full of courage, joy, and imagination, as demonstrated by a tumultuous history in which social and political changes have taken place at such a pace that all classes of the population, both rich and poor, were involved.
Representing all of this meant seeking a liberating crescendo for which the natural setting was the massive Zocalo Square, in which independence was celebrated for a huge crowd and for many heads of state, and the emblems of the country converged with both tradition and innovation. Fire and strength, but also iconography and art, were the founding symbols employed to honor the memory of a population that has never forgotten the values of independence as well as a commitment against poverty, a desire to rebel against a coercive society, and the satisfaction awarded by a strong sense of national belonging.

Preparations for the ceremony, which involved as many as six hundred people, began with a series of rehearsals in the fascinating location where the Teotihuacan pyramids stand, a mystical place linked to the ancient Mexican civilizations, which welcomed, in the days leading to the bicentennial celebrations, dozens of ethnic groups, with costumes and languages that bore witness to their origin.
A massive daytime parade expressing the ideal of a momentous change was a call to a collective celebration that mobilized two million people across Mexico City. Fire and dragons, heroes that shaped the country's history, and icons such as Frida Kahlo and Diego Rivera, among others, were the ingredients for creating a ceremony in which the culture and strength of the Mexican popular tradition were the focus for an engaging and adventurous event, spectacular in the true sense of the term, but above all anthropologically truthful. The images it left behind still evoke the powerful visions and sounds of this monumental national celebration.

Síntesis de
DIARIO DE MEXICO
Del Domingo 16 de septiembre de 1810
¡Mexicanos!
¡Mexicanos!
¡Mexicanos!
va MEXICO!
¡Viva MEXICO!
¡Viva Morelos!
¡Viva Hidalgo!
¡Viva Allende!
¡Viva Aldama!
gidora!
¡Viva La Corr
MEXICO
2010

"I still feel a
connection
with them."

Walking into that huge, beautiful stadium was almost overwhelming, but looking across the flag at the other very special, accomplished women who also shared this honor was moving in another lasting way. I still feel a connection with them.

Susan Sarandon

A PIAZZA UNDER THE SEA

America's Cup World Series Opening

A ceremony celebrating the sea, in which the symbols chosen to express emotions and meaning are of crucial importance, Piazza del Plebiscito in Naples was the setting for a ceremony presenting the America's Cup and its international values. The square was transformed into the ideal stage for the narration of a story about the sea and the boats that cross it, thanks to the skillful combination of light, colors, words, and sounds that placed the great tradition of this city at the heart of the event.

Rain poured down on the ceremony, but not one actor, sailor, representative of the authorities, or member of the audience left the show in which everyone felt involved, in one of the most beautiful cities in the world. The ceremony for the America's Cup World Series exalted the spirit of the America's Cup, revealing the historical tradition uniting cities such as Barcelona, Rio de Janeiro, San Diego, Auckland, and Naples, in an ideal journey honoring competition and the most acclaimed names in this sporting event. Italian legends were included such as *Azzurra,* which competed to win the Cup in 1987, or *Il Moro di Venezia*, another famed boat built by Raoul Gardini, or *Luna Rossa*, a

five-time contender for the America's Cup, part of the history of sailing.

Prestigious institutional representatives, such as Italian president Giorgio Napolitano, who gave a speech on video, and high-ranking officers from the Italian navy took part in the celebrations.

This combination of protocol and sport was framed by Naples' beauty and culture, from the words of Eduardo De Filippo to the stunning architecture of Piazza del Plebiscito, lit with masterful skill, to a theatrical representation of marine life; the city watched the athletes' teams march in a show of light and words that was designed to communicate the values of the America's Cup.

It was a ceremony that had the responsibility of representing Italy to the whole world, and a production that was put to the test by extreme weather conditions; a magical evening in which the values of sailing aroused the enthusiasm of an audience, passionate about this prestigious award and its celebrated history.

D·O·M·D·FRANCISCO·DE·PAVLA·FERDINANDVS·REX·VOTO·A·MDCCCXVI

D·O·M·D FRANCISCO

VI A FERDINANDVS I EX VOTO A MDCCCXVI

AMERICA'S
CUP

"Working with Marco Balich is
a breathtaking challenge."

Working with Marco Balich is an exciting privilege as well as a breathtaking challenge. We worked together for the first time during the opening ceremony of the Torino 2006 Winter Olympics. Adrenaline was running high; it was my first performance in a stadium, and conditions were particularly difficult: a massive space with no reference points, a floor that was not designed for dancing, frigid temperatures, and a world-wide live TV broadcast to top it all.

Marco, however, has the ability to allow you to give your best while granting you complete creative freedom, and to enhance the result with a spectacular and impeccable staging that makes each gesture exponentially stronger and more striking.

It was an unforgettable experience both on a personal level, and for the world of dance as a whole, which for the first time had such a prestigious role within an Olympic opening ceremony.

I believe this was also a great opportunity for our country to show to the entire world an important element of our art and culture, of which I have always been proud to be an ambassador. Marco Balich was able to conceive a daring and dazzling mix between dance and Olympic games, all the more extraordinary for its cultural implications.

Roberto Bolle

EVERYMAN'S CAR

New Fiat 500 World Premiere

"Welcome 500" was an invitation ushering in a piece of Italy, not only in terms of car design, but also of the social history of a country as a whole, from the 1950s to the present day.

The show began with the unmistakable sound of an engine starting, the legendary car that Italy has come to know so well. When it was designed, this invention gave Italians the possibility of freedom, of running toward a future full of hope. The show took place entirely on the River Po, a way to link the history of Turin with that of the entire country.

On the river, scenes of daily life, of sea and sport, of struggle and dreams floated by, a narration unwinding on the notes of "Dolce Vita" that Fellini traced indelibly in the world's collective memory. Nothing could be more desirable than the icon of Anita Ekberg, aloof and out of reach, in a costume that skimmed the surface of the water, demonstrating that this country is just as capable of talking about poetry as they are about industrial design, revisiting with the New Fiat 500 a symbol that dates back fifty years: a car for the people, by the people.

Meanwhile, images of an economic boom that transformed this country, also thanks to cinema, music, theater, and painting flowed along the river crossing Turin, the definitive Italian industrial city, and the ideal location to pay homage to a legend such as the first Fiat 500. Evocative images followed one another: the Beatles, Marilyn Monroe, and finally a beautiful 500 in the shape of a cake, the last romantic scene before the show transformed into something else.

The next part of the celebration kicked off with a tribute to technology and the aspirations of a new industrial destiny. A steel structure representing a car was lowered onto the stage, carrying performers who flew, jumped, and bounced with renewed energy. The music speeded up, evoking a kind of hyper-space in which the country's past receded as its future and collective determination to develop grew.

The new 500 became the perfect metaphor of a young and vital world, wishing to speed ahead full steam without relinquishing the possibility of dreaming, as those who once created this legendary car have thought.

GR 8000

"A whole
life
condensed
into
an hour."

One evening the Juventus team and its supporters opened their eyes and found themselves deep into their history, their emotions, their tears and joy. It was a whole life condensed into an hour: thinking about it, it was incredible.

The opening of the Juventus Stadium influenced our competitive and professional journey, marking its fate for many years to come. Our hard work, the resources we invested, and our passion needed a spark, and that evening the fire of a new history began to burn. It was almost magical.

Andrea Agnelli

CELEBRATING VENICE

A Sensational Carnival - New Year's Eve - Festa del Redentore

Years of work and two original formats went into representing the emotions, visions, and dreams, in a city among the most beautiful in the world, the best training ground for the creation of diverse and unexpected events. Three editions of Carnival and two editions of the New Year's Eve celebrations and of the *Festa del Redentore* were designed for the city of Venice; each of them was a very special event, welcomed with enthusiasm by the audience.

For Venice's *Carnevale*, one of the most famous and celebrated carnivals in the world, a new format linked to the six senses was developed. Each sense corresponded to one of the *sestieri*, the six districts of Venice, creating new ways of perceiving the urban space that enabled the audience to discover the millenary history of this unique city. Thus Dorsoduro was touch, Santa Croce smell, Cannaregio taste, Castello hearing, and San Polo sight, while San Marco represented the sixth sense: intuition, symbolized by an iconic brain. Different forms of narration had a common denominator: wonder and beauty, as in a reinterpretation of traditions in which San Marco square was transformed into a Renaissance garden, or the historical "Flight of the Angel" was performed for the first time by a man.

A collaboration with Milan's Institute for the Blind brought to Venice the successful format of *Dialogue in the Dark*, giving participants the opportunity to experience the world without seeing it, and added a new, more touching and emotional dimension to the usual merriment of Carnival.

The *Festa del Redentore* is a festival taking place every year in July, which connects Venice to its history and traditions, and more specifically commemorates the order given by the Venetian senate in 1576 to build the church of the *Redentore*, the Redeemer, to give thanks for the end of a plague that had been devastating the city, killing tens of thousands of people.

Five centuries of history were thus the starting point for a celebration that followed the tradition of this classic Venetian event, but also opened up the scenic space for the *foghi*, the fireworks that are the most characteristic feature of this event. The lagoon was enveloped by a pyrotechnic display that filled the city's skies and created scenes of an almost pictorial quality.

Finally, the central theme for the New Year's Eve celebrations was Love: the audience was invited to stage a collective midnight kiss in one of the most romantic cities in the world, the ideal setting for visions capable of captivating thousands of people.

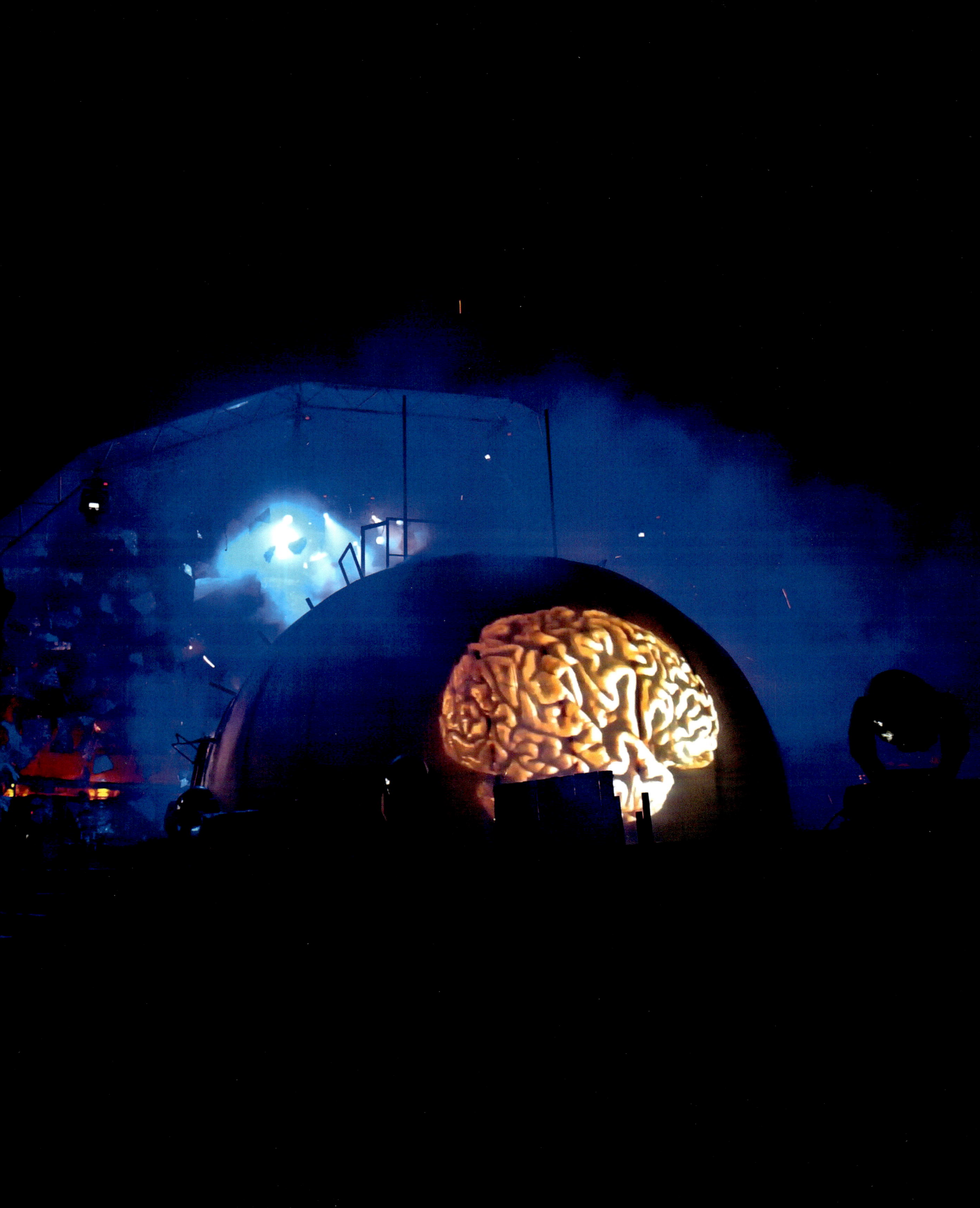

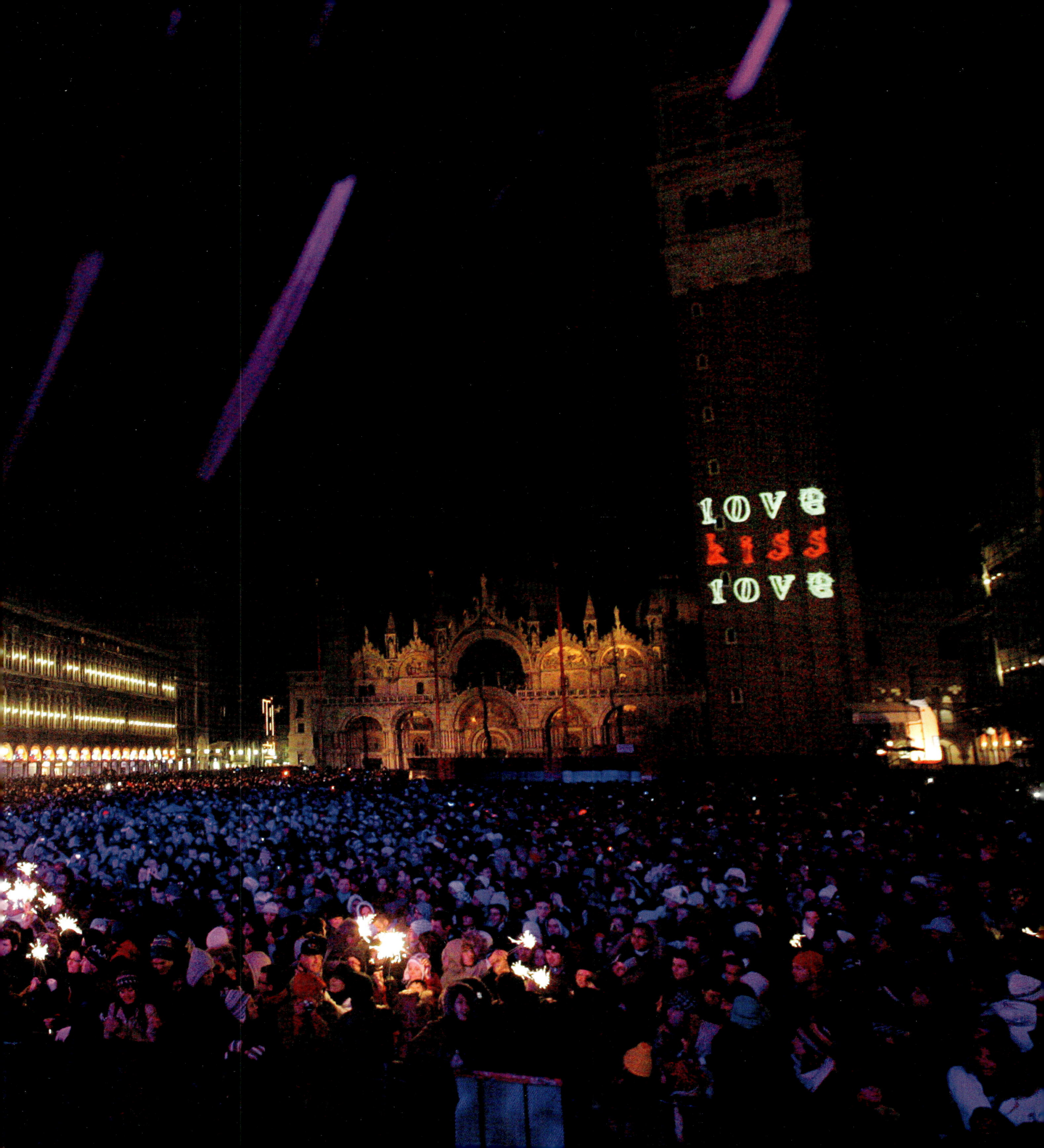
love
kiss
love

Museo Correr
Depero

EZIA

"Carrying the
Olympic flag
with seven
extraordinary
women was a
wonderful
privilege."

Taking part in the Olympic games in Turin was a great honor for me, and it still is an important memory in my career. The message of peace that the Olympics bring to the world is an example for our youth and for all those who wish for a brighter future for everybody.

I give credit to Marco Balich's direction for representing Italy at its best with a ceremony that truly moved me.

Carrying the Olympic flag with seven extraordinary women was a wonderful privilege. I remember with admiration my fellow flagbearers, with whcm I have had the pleasure of marching in the stadium: Isabel Allende, Manuela di Centa, Maria De Lurdes Mutola, Nawal El Moutawakel, Somaly Mam, Wangari Maathai, and Susan Sarandon. It was a very important moment for me and for all the women of the world.

Sophia Loren

LOVE FOREVER

A Fairy Tale Wedding

India is a generous land, as is Puglia, smaller but just as welcoming thanks to its scents and sounds, its spirituality, and its magnificent natural landscapes. The southern Italian region, then, was the ideal setting for an extraordinary wedding, a celebration of exceptional beauty lasting three days.

Props, costumes, and projections were created to allow the bride and groom, their families, and their guests, to share the unique emotions that are linked to such a significant moment in life.

Moving a staff of dozens of people and bringing hundreds of guests from all over the world required a great organizational and creative energy. It was a production that put together a complex combination of elements, from the food, referencing the culture of the couple's origin, to music, colors, technologically innovative costumes, and flower decorations; the latter, an essential basis of a wedding party, needing to seamlessly integrate with the ancient olive trees dotting the Puglia landscape.

A boat on the river and a bright full moon, part of an iconography connected to the ceremony's content, opened an unforgettable celebration. Among the olive trees that watched over as the history of this land unfolded, the guests were treated to epic reenactments of the myths of Ancient Greece and to a fairy tale atmosphere reminiscent of the Italian town of Bomarzo and its visionary gardens. The technology that animated props and costumes was also a symbolic tribute to contemporary India, a country that is developing at an increasing pace.

Finally the Cosmos, portrayed as a space of spirituality where dreamy figures were made to dance, was the theme that brought the celebrations to a conclusion and initiated a lasting journey of love, a solid value in any religion or philosophy on the planet. The memory and magic of this event still resonate in the hearts of the bride and groom and of everyone involved—all, for three unforgettable days, surrounded by images of breathtaking beauty.

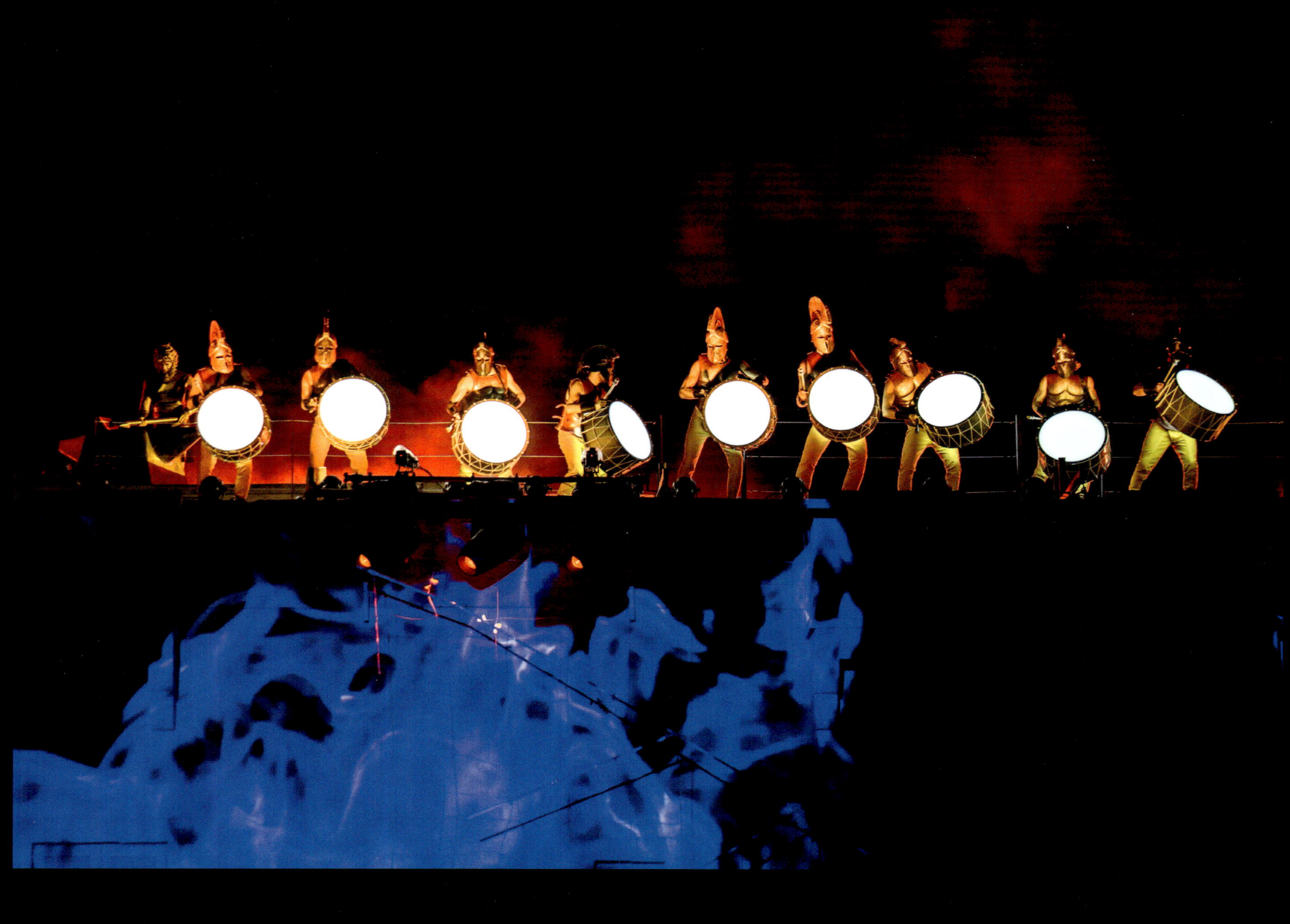

ika
&
ghan

"The triumph of the human spirit"

The opening and closing ceremonies of the Paralympic Games—summer or winter—should go beyond the amazing performances of the athletes during the Games and really get down to the true philosophical messages that Paralympians subconsciously project when they perform. The values that are exhibited in the ceremonies that Marco has directed celebrate the triumph of the human spirit fighting against, and knocking down, obstacles that are placed in the way of the personal development of many individuals all over the world.

In the Torino 2006 Paralympics, with the opening ceremony's main concept being "Breaking All Limits, Breaking All Barriers," there was a very "in-your-face" representation of individuals tearing down barriers in a somewhat violent way. It was a physical representation of a feeling that takes over people's minds and hearts when they are stopped from developing their own lives by historically out-of-date philosophies. It is the very experience of both ceremonies and Paralympians' performances that rid us of these antiquated ideas and leave only positivity moving forward.

In the Paralympic closing ceremony of Sochi 2014, an incredible message was sent by the video game blocks being transformed by the amazing human achievement of the rope climber, from something being impossible to that individual and many individuals all over the world saying "I'm Possible." This brought together everything that freedom represents: freedom of the heart, freedom of the mind, and freedom of the body, leading to freedom of the spirit.

All the ceremonies that Marco has been involved with have been quite different from each other, but they have all revolved around a common and crucial theme, which is, as was said in Atlanta in 1996, "The Triumph of the Human Spirit," and that I would now term in 2014 "The Liberation of an Incredible Human Spirit for the Betterment of the World." I think that this is something that is right at the heart of everything that Marco does, and I am sure will continue to do, as we move forward and our paths hopefully cross on many occasions in the future.

Sir Philip Craven

Passion lives here

PASSION LIVES HERE

Torino 2006 Olympic and Paralympic Ceremonies

Humankind was at the center of a fascinating ceremony that paid tribute to progress. The industrial city of Turin was celebrated by a narration filled with passion and rhythm, dynamism and magnificence. Even the audience were dressed in white as a reference to the mountain landscapes where the games took place.

The show kicked off with the great Olympic champion Jury Chechi wielding a hammer and sparking the enthusiasm of the whole stadium as he forcefully hit an anvil. Fire animated the ceremony thanks to the "red skaters," athletes who carried a flame on their heads and brought life to a pulsating heart made by hundreds of dancers in a breathtaking choreography.

The ceremony's narrative power evoked the cultural heritage of the Renaissance and the short twentieth century, the time in which industrial modernity was born. This era was interpreted by Roberto Bolle, a world-class dancer who pitted himself against machines in the shape of giant dancers, moved by performers on the field of play. A scene in which music and power merged, while the renowned sculpture by Umberto Boccioni, *Unique Forms of Continuity in Space*, represented a transition from the grace of the human body to the concept of pure technology embodied by a Ferrari car, a symbol of Italian design.

The Olympic flag entered the stadium, carried, for the first time, by an all-female group of flag bearers, including personalities such as Susan Sarandon, Sophia Loren, and Isabel Allende, in a celebration of all women. The flag's entrance was followed by the aerial performance of acrobats who created an enchanting human "Dove of Peace." Yoko Ono's speech quoting the words of "Imagine" led into Luciano Pavarotti's last live appearance, in a proscenium representing Italian opera and its great success in the world.

In the closing ceremony the tension melted, giving way to a festival of absolute joy. It was an "Italian Carnival" that welcomed the tired bodies of the athletes and carried the audience in a whirl of history, with references to traditional characters such as Pulcinella and Harlequin, or hints of the world of *Alice in Wonderland*. The culture of theater, of funambulists, of the Italian farce, finally took over and turned the ceremony into a lively party.

The opening ceremony of the Torino Paralympics made no concession to the rhetoric of disability, but rather offered a civil answer to a need for equality.

A great staircase standing as a wall in the middle of the stadium was torn down by a giant wheelchair. A moving performance by Simona Atzori, a dancer with no arms, told the story of a normality that is always potentially within reach, especially with courage. Once and for all, able people and people with disabilities were closer than ever.

In the last 20 years I have published a few books, but I have lived in anonymity until February of 2006, when I carried the Olympic flag in the Winter Olympics in Italy. That made me a celebrity. Now people recognize me in Macy's, and my grandchildren think that I'm cool.

Allow me to tell you about my four minutes of fame. One of the organizers of the Olympic ceremony, of the opening ceremony, called me and said that I had been selected to be one of the flagbearers. I replied that surely this was a case of mistaken identity because I'm as far as you can get from being an athlete. Actually, I wasn't even sure that I could go around the stadium without a walker. I was told that this was no laughing matter. This would be the first time that only women would carry the Olympic flag. Five women, representing five continents, and three Olympic gold medal winners.

"The best four minutes of my entire life

By the middle of February, I found myself in Turin, where enthusiastic crowds cheered when any of the eighty Olympic teams was in the street. Those athletes had sacrificed everything to compete in the games. They all deserved to win, but there's the element of luck. A speck of snow, an inch of ice, the force of the wind can determine the result of a race or a game. However, what matters most—more than training or luck—is the heart. Only a fearless and determined heart will get the gold medal. It is all about passion. The streets of Turin were covered with red posters announcing the slogan of the Olympics.

Passion lives here. Isn't it always true? Heart is what drives us and determines our fate. In the green room of the stadium, I met the other flag bearers: three athletes and the actresses Susan Sarandon and Sophia Loren. Also, two women with passionate hearts: Wangari Maathai, the Nobel prizewinner from Kenya who has planted thirty million trees. And by doing so, she has changed the soil, the weather in some places in Africa, and of course the economic conditions in many villages. And Somaly Mam, a Cambodian activist who fights passionately against child prostitution.

In the green room I received my uniform. It was not the kind of outfit that I normally wear, but it was far from the Michelin Man suit that I had anticipated. Not bad, really. I looked like a refrigerator. But so did most of the flag bearers, except Sophia Loren, the universal symbol of beauty and passion. Sophia is over seventy and she looks great. When asked in a TV interview, "How could she look so good?" She replied, "Posture. My back is always straight, and I don't make old people's noises."

At some point around midnight, we were summoned to the wings of the stadium, and

were those in the Olympic stadium."

the loudspeakers announced the Olympic flag, and the music started. Sophia Loren was right in front of me—she's a foot taller than I am, not counting the poofy hair. She walked elegantly, like a giraffe on the African savannah, holding the flag on her shoulder. I jogged behind—on my tiptoes—holding the flag on my extended arm, so that my head was actually under the damn flag. All the cameras were, of course, on Sophia. That was fortunate for me, because in most press photos I appear too, although often between Sophia's legs—a place where most men would love to be.

The best four minutes of my entire life were those in the Olympic stadium.

Isabel Allende

UNEARTHING GREATNESS

Celebrating FC Shakhtar

The story begins in the mines that for a long time have formed the backbone of this region. Things have changed in Ukraine, but in a not too distant past the destiny of thousands of people was bound to that of the mines, from which coal and other minerals necessary for the development of the country were extracted. This was the starting point for the opening of the Donbass Arena, the new stadium of FC Shakhtar, a tough, solid football team which has shown great success in European competitions, as well as for the ceremony celebrating the team s seventy-fifth anniversary. Both ceremonies, one staged in 2009 and one in 2011, featured hundreds of performers dressed as miners dancing on the field of play, as a tribute to the history of these lands. During the Donbass Arena opening, a composition of thousands of helmets on the stadium's ground, brought to mind a past that has laid the foundations for the values of this country.

The succession of events in these ceremonies aimed at representing in a spectacular way local rituals and traditions, with dance performances and music that are famous the world over. The turning point in the first of the two ceremonies was the landing of a UFO carrying a team of aliens bent on brutally conquering Earth. The Shakhtar players were not fazed, and with football tricks that startled a group of increasingly furious aliens, won the game—a symbolic match against violence that hints at how, in this region, political issues are far from being resolved in terms of boundaries and fundamental freedoms.

In the second ceremony, a large hill loomed over a small football field, the emblem of a history of struggle and competition, a combination that is quite often invincible.

Today the Shakhtar champions are legendary figures who have reaped prestigious honors on the field, and this is all that matters. The ceremony commemorating the team's seventy-fifth anniversary featured a parade of some of these legends, who received a rightfully earned tribute to their personal histories, as well as to that of their city.

It was a well-deserved double celebration of a team and its future aspirations. Seventy-five years of history are a significant achievement, as is the building of a new and welcoming stadium to receive rival teams and maybe, when needed, to treat them as invading aliens.

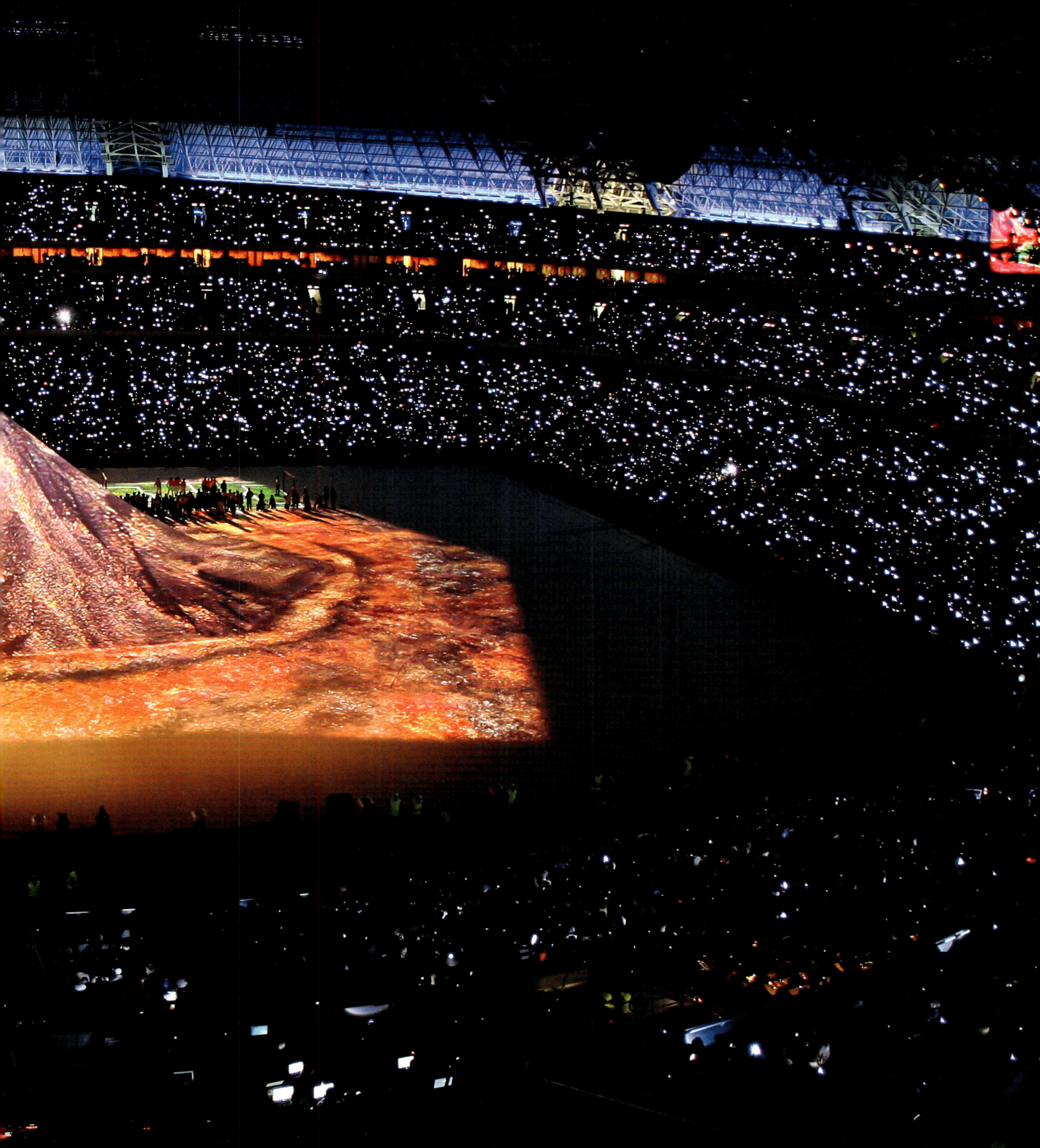

CAFE   MUSEUM   FAN SHOP

A FOOTBALL SYMPHONY

UEFA Euro 2012 Ceremonies

The opening and closing ceremonies of the UEFA Euro 2012 Games united Ukraine and Poland in a metaphor summoning the highest values of sport: just like different instruments and tunes play together and create a magnificent symphony, football teams from all over Europe met, giving birth to a great tournament.

The Euro 2012 Games involved eight locations in both countries, which provided the setting for a thrilling competition, represented by a simple and equally powerful symbol: a flower, that thanks to a large-scale inflatable, came to life in the Warsaw stadium in the final scene of the opening ceremony. The value of these ceremonies is contained in the petals of this emblem, designed to communicate a sense of trust, fair competition, and above all, respect for others, the fundamental value upon which any sporting tournaments should be founded.

The opening began with strips of fabric cascading from above toward the field of play, in a representation of the flags of the two host countries. They were immediately followed by the entrance of hundreds of volunteers who animated the stadium with a colorful performance.

Local cultural history was fittingly celebrated by remembering the Polish origins of one of the most renowned classical composers of all time: Frédéric Chopin. One of his compositions was played on a piano at the center of the field, and was then mixed with the contemporary tunes of a DJ. While the pianist revealed unexpected footballing skills, the volunteers broke into an irresistible choreography.

The word "respect" was written in giant letters on the audience stands, moments before the giant logo of the games was displayed in the stadium, to the audience's amazement.

In the closing ceremony in Kiev a colorful mass choreography highlighted the importance of the Games' final challenge. A large-scale symbolic match united athletes and supporters in an ideal global world in which sport can teach humanity how to progress toward a future of peace.

FIFA
WARSAW
adidas SHARP
2012
GREECE
UEFA.com

UEFA EURO 2012
THE FINAL

"Marco
is a
born
organizer."

Marco Balich is a born organizer. If Napoleon had let him organize the battle of Waterloo he would have surely wor.

His ability to stage these extravaganzas stems from an impressive mix of elements, but above all from two things: the fact that he is from Venice, and that he learned his trade in Milan in the 1980s, when the city was a hub of creativity and business savvy. He did the rest, with his ability to let images flow and bring people together without ever saying "It can't be done," apart from when it is actually true. Every time I have worked with Marco Balich I have admired this great talent of his, and even when I wasn't directly involved I applauded him as a fan.

Lorenzo Cherubini

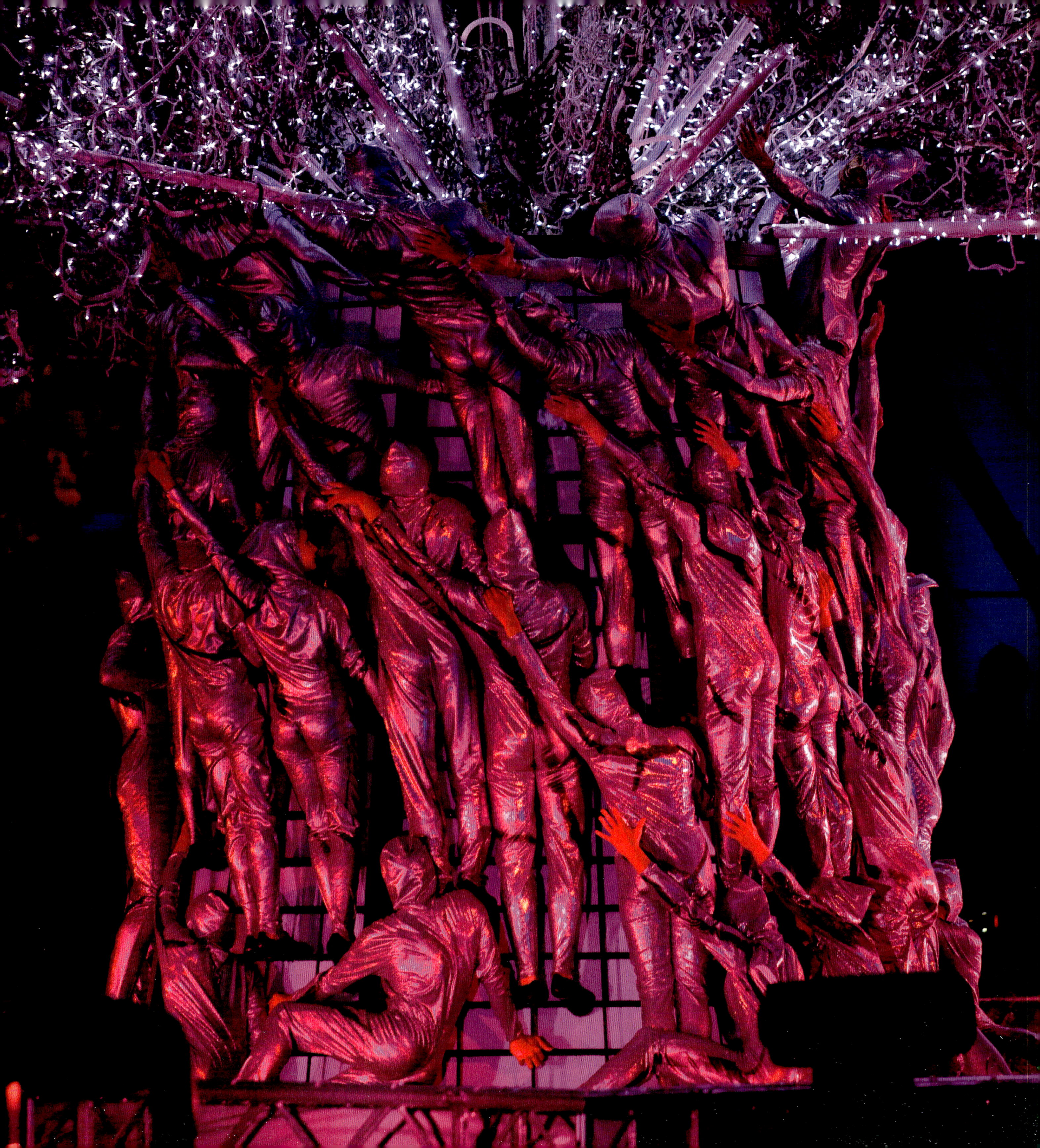

THE JOURNEY OF WATER

The ceremony began with a provocative countdown in which a flock of sheep marked the seconds separating us from the official start of the games.

In fact, this edition of the Mediterranean Games honored, in a positive and solemn way, the victims of the earthquake that turned the city of L'Aquila to rubble. The Italian flag arrived, carried by firemen, modest heroes called to take part in the opening ceremony precisely to show the citizens of L'Aquila that they had not been forgotten by civil society.

A stage at the center of the Pescara stadium was the ideal proscenium toward the Mediterranean and its journeys of memory.

Hundreds of volunteers filled the field of play, paying tribute to the natural qualities and potential of the Mediterranean diet with beautiful costumes representing wheat, peppers, and vegetables of all sorts, while a giant fork symbolized the deliciousness of the cuisine from this region.

A homage to Gabriele D'Annunzio, born in Pescara, and to his love Ermione, was the prologue to a touching performance by ballet *étoile* Eleonora Abbagnato and to the entrance of the athletes, the true protagonists of the games. The atmosphere was joyful and filled with historical references, such as during the ap-

pearance of the "Warrior of Capestrano," a local symbol depicting a soldier from the ancient Italic population of the Picentes. The huge statue was raised on the field of play, representing the noble memory of the places to which the ceremony brought new life with a spectacle of dance, color, and sound.

A journey across the Mediterranean region portrayed the symbols connected to the water washing its shores. And water was the link to a more recent history: a mother and her child, born during the earthquake in L'Aquila, symbolized new beginnings, the source of which was the "Fountain of the 99 Spouts," a famous monument of this devastated city. The water was taken to the stadium in Pescara and poured into an amphora, emblematic of motherhood and symbolic strength in which human beings find a common purpose towards peace and prosperity.

The closing ceremony of the games took thousands of white-robed people to the beach, giving voice to a clear and concrete message that unified all people who live on the Mediterranean, including those who have not yet found peace.

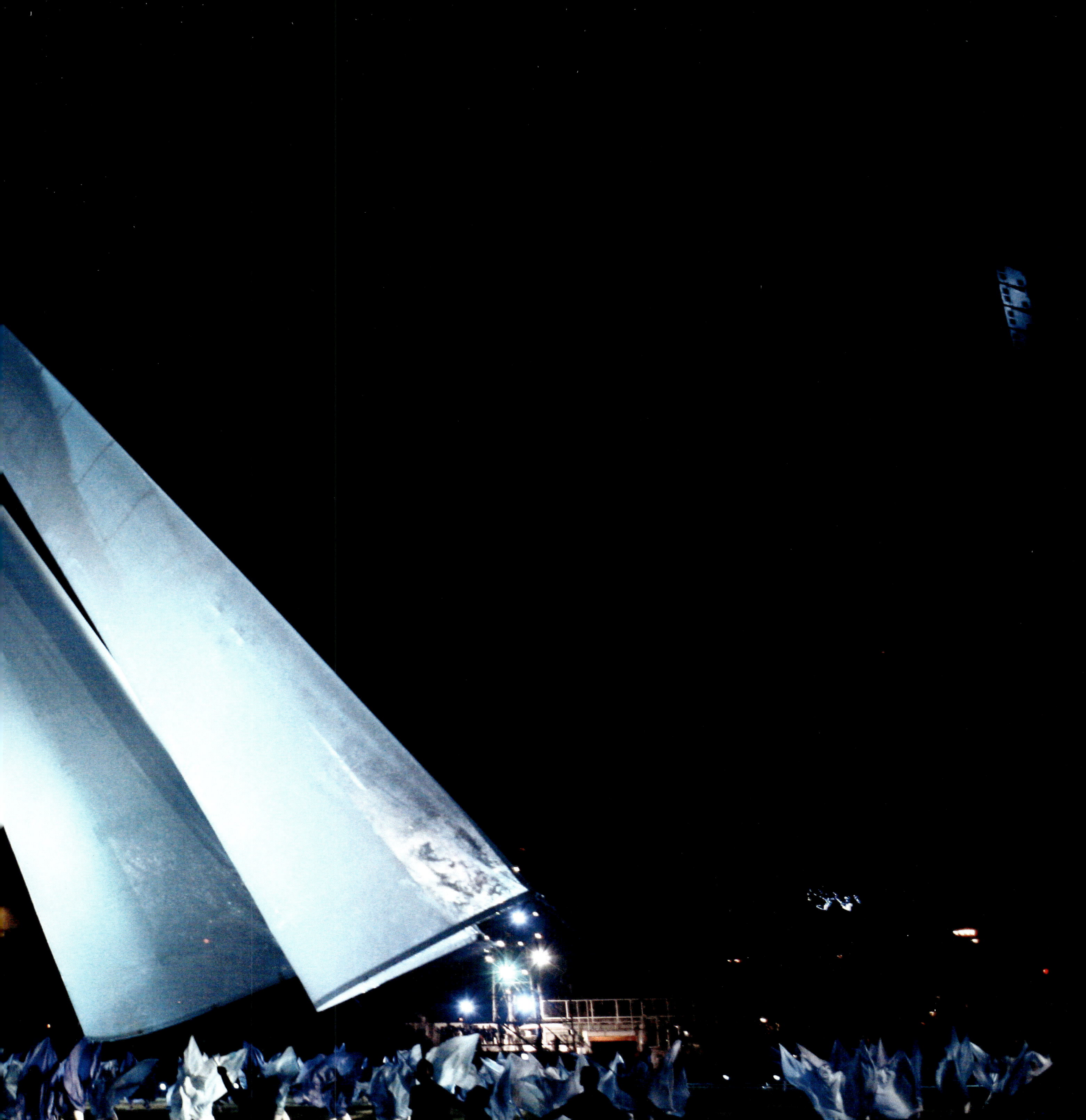

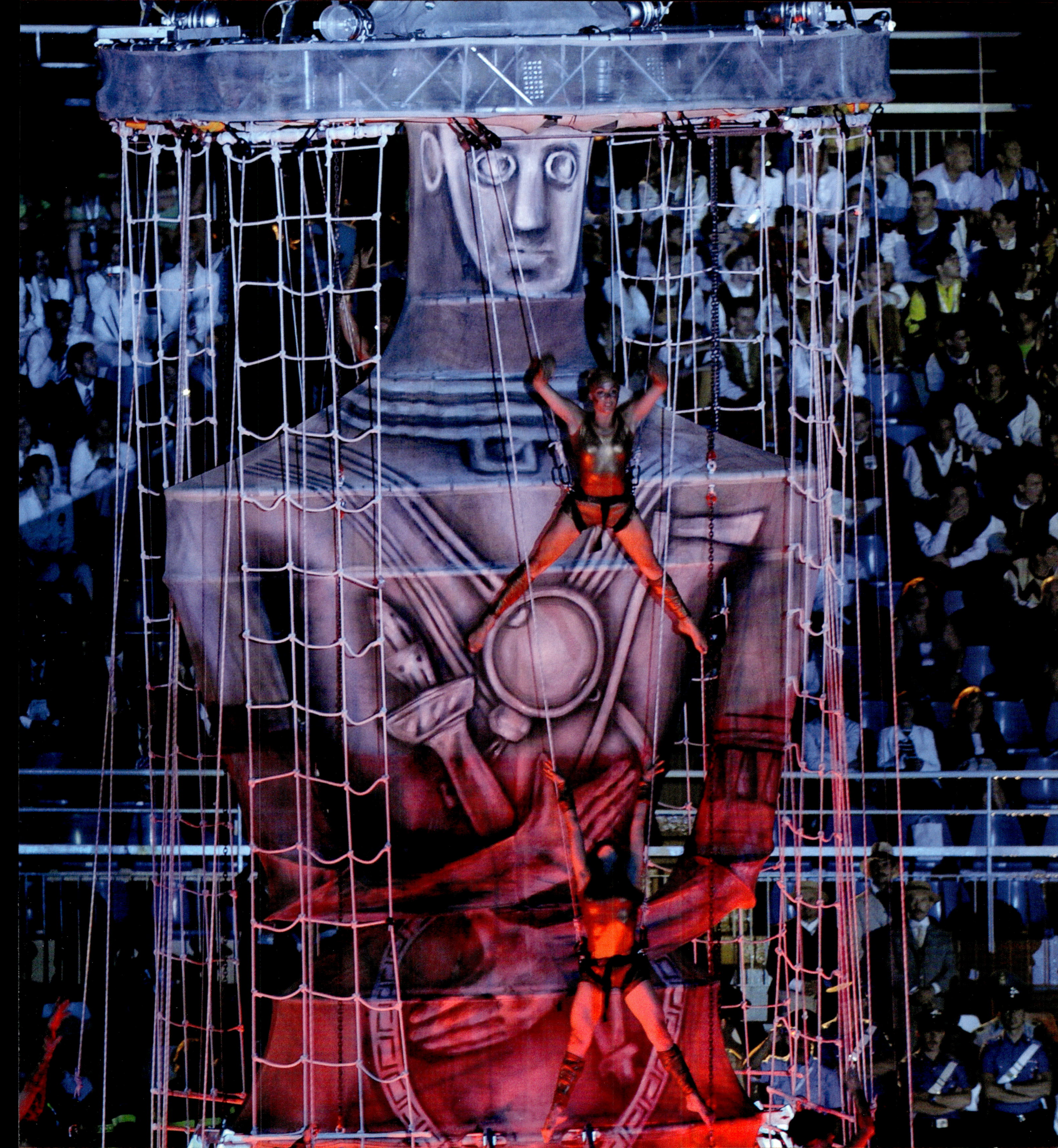

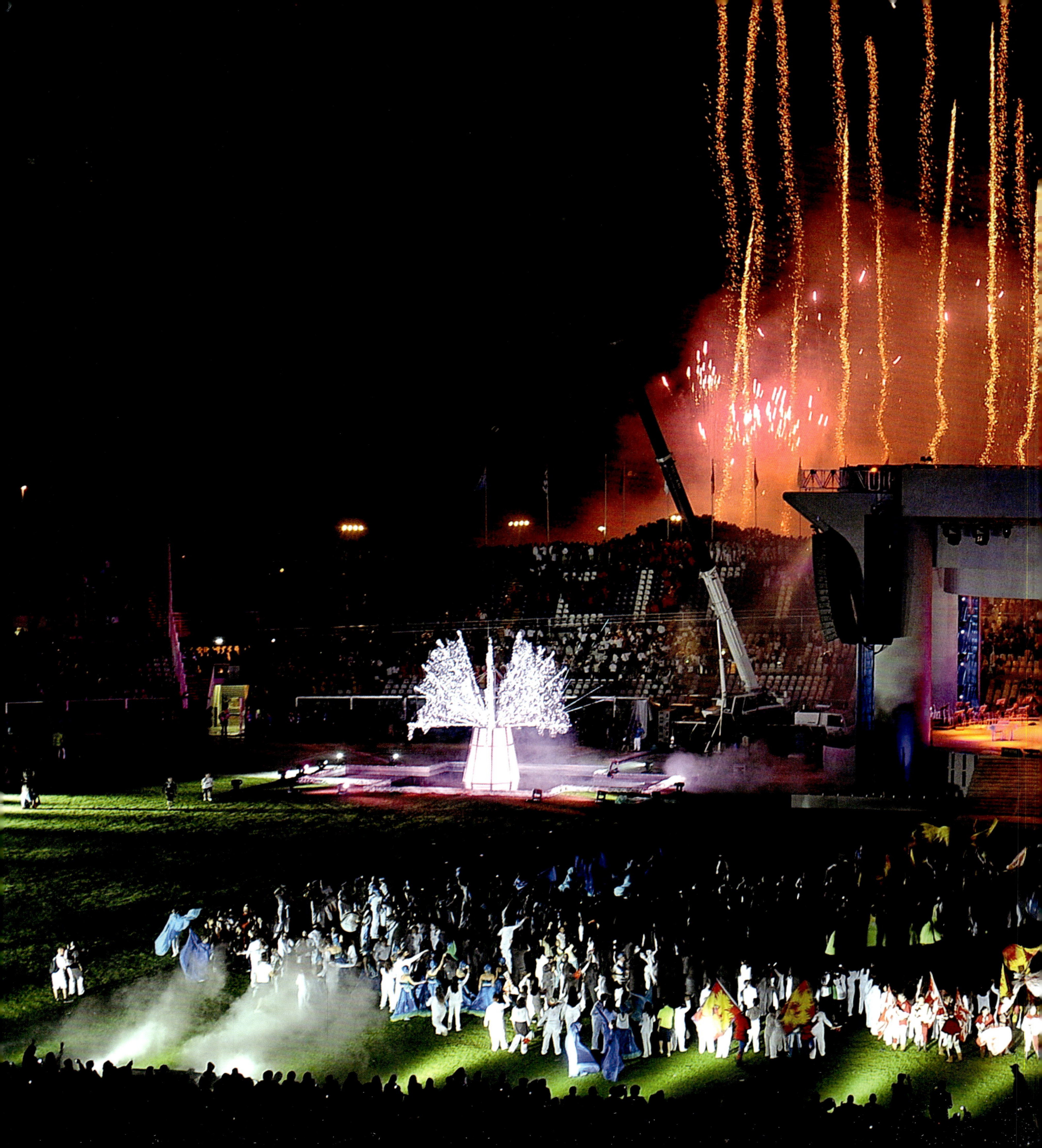

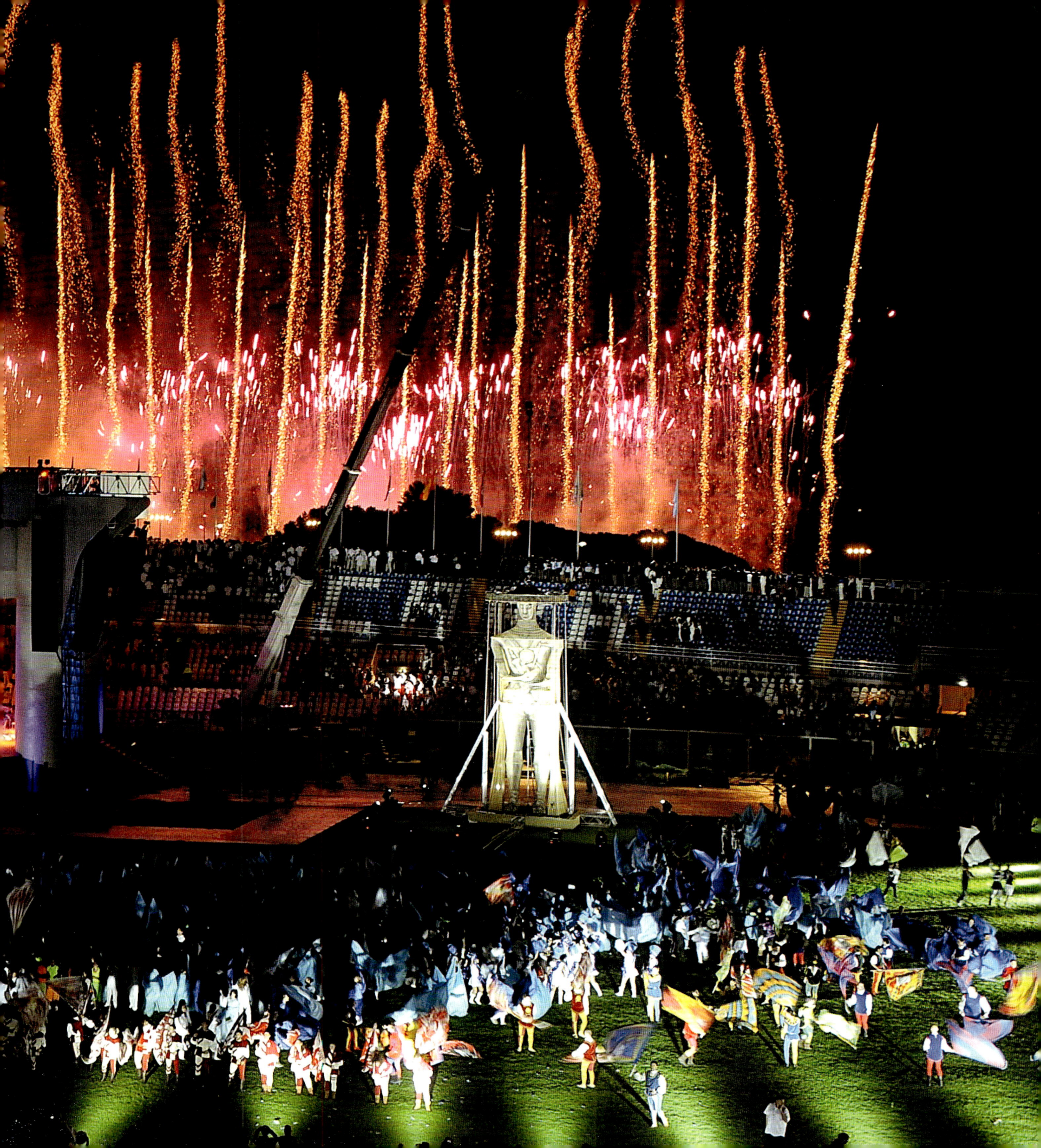

"A totally new and
rewarding experience"

Many years have gone by since I worked for the Winter Olympics in Turin, appointed by Marco Balich and Lida Castelli, and yet I can still recall a feeling of great pride.

Not only were all of us on the team aware that we were taking part in one of the most prestigious international events, but we all shared the satisfaction of being professionally and creatively impeccable, as well as a sense of responsibility, symbolic but also very tangible. We worked hard, but the fantastic atmosphere that Marco and Lida were able to create allowec us to do so without feeling pressured, and in fact it was a really fun experience.

Personally, I tried to offer my expertise while taking in the advice and needs of the professionals involved, who I could interact with directly during rehearsals, something that does not usually happen in film productions. My aim was to design costumes that enhanced the performers' movements and by doing so complemented the show's creative direction.

Taking part in this event was for me a totally new and rewarding professional experience, which gave me the opportunity to explore uncharted territories for my career.

Gabriella Pescucci

WELCOME HOME

Juventus Stadium Opening

At the end of the countdown that always opens a ceremony, inspiring rhythm and enthusiasm in the audience, the evening kicked off with three black-and-white giraffes entering the new stadium of Juventus, one of the most awarded teams in the world.

The three giraffes launched into a wild dance, while around them dozens of percussionists built up the energy already running high among the fans on the stands.

Minute by minute, the number of performers on the field increased, and footballs started invading the scene. Everyone moved to the rhythm of the drums, waving flags and drawing black-and-white patterns, an homage to the hosts of this special evening.

Hundreds of performers created luminous, fleeting chiaroscuro effects, fast and sudden, representing finally an enormous "1897," the club's founding year, followed by the number "6," a tribute to the unforgettable champion Gaetano Scirea. Immediately afterwards an acrobat flew above the audience, carried by a mass of helium balloons that lent infinite grace to her movements.

The concept of flight was the underlying theme of this ceremony, a flight of the imagination, suspended between yesterday and today, the size of the stadium in time and space, treating the audience to a series of beautifully moving scenes, such as the bench flying in from the sky, on which sat Giampiero Boniperti and Alessandro Del Piero, two absolute stars from the team: a reference to the history of the Juventus team, which started on that same bench decades before.

Another symbolic flight in the ceremony recalled a bygone era: two children representing the young Gianni and Umberto Agnelli were lifted up, in an embrace that extended to Juventus and to the whole city.

No less important was the memory of the incidents that took place in the Heysel stadium in Belgium on May 29, 1985 during the Champions League final between Juventus and Liverpool, when thirty-nine people died, the majority Italian supporters. This was a fundamental moment of remembrance, included in this ceremony to remind us that emotions, even sad ones, cannot be left out of a day of celebration such as this.

In the evening's final sequence, hundreds of volunteers with glowing costumes outlined three stars representing the thirty championships won by Juventus, then a luminous Italian flag and finally the words pronounced by Andrea Agnelli, the young president of the team who embodies its present history: "Welcome Home."

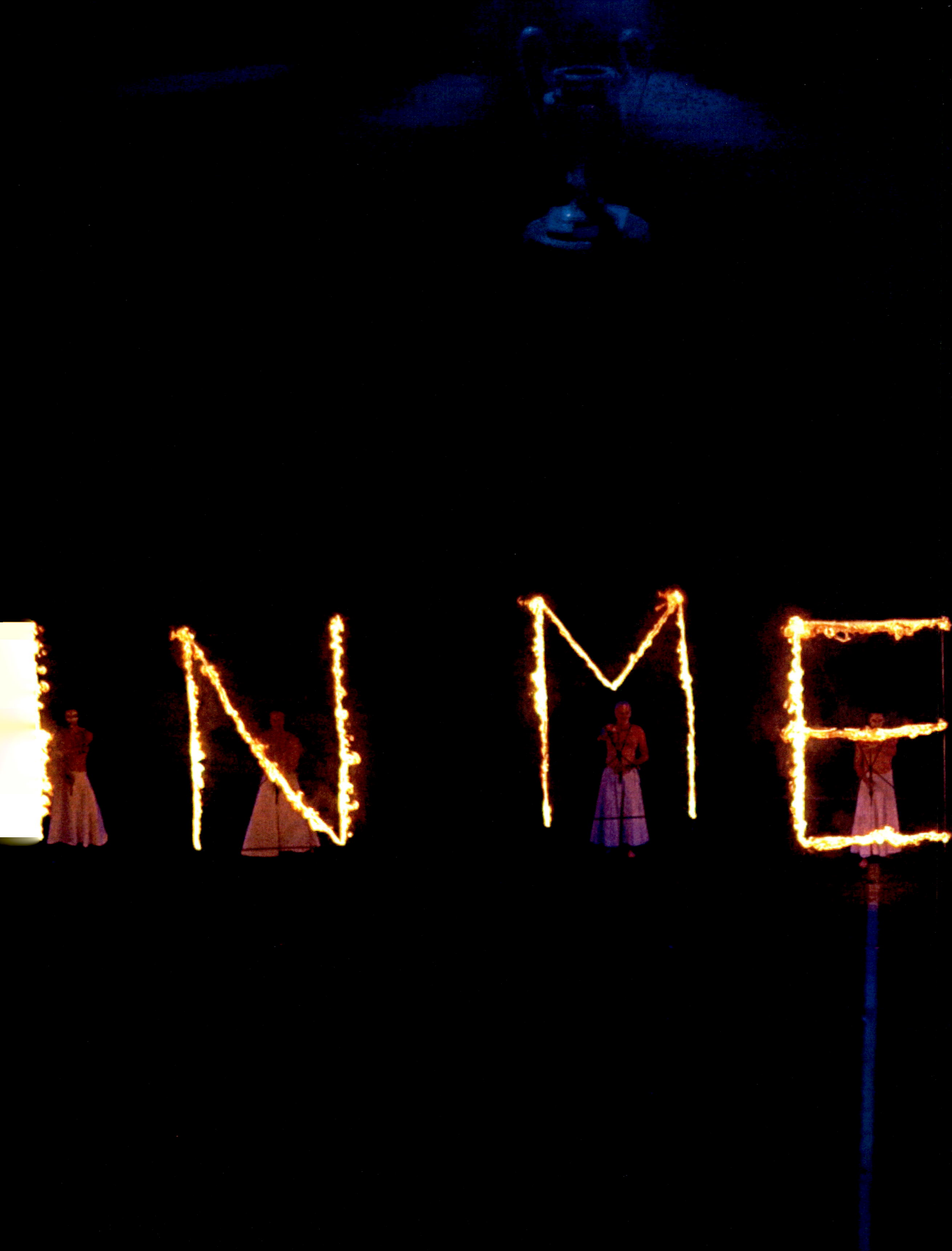
IN ME

MORY

"Talent, imagination, inventiveness."

Marco Balich's creativity has the power to make you dream, to amaze you. His creations have the same exhilarating effect as a penalty shot, during which you hold your breath whle the ball flies higher and higher, and then enters the goal. Talent, imagination, inventiveness. But also hard work and pragmatism.

I owe Marco Balich one of my favorite memories on the football pitch. It wasn't a match, but the opening ceremony of the Juventus football stadium on September 8, 2011, of which he was the creator. Giampiero Boniperti and I were standing on the field, and from the sky a bench came flying in, the same one on which more than a century before a few young students founded the club.

"Your moment must be, and will be, the most moving of the whole evening." Those were the words spoken by Marco, who wanted to appeal to our emotional and spontaneous side, while all around us each element in the show was flawlessly organized and impeccably polished. He spoke to me in a straightforward manner, as all great people do, making the organization of an event that is a perfect yet extremely complex machine appear easy.

I am very happy to have worked with a great Italian talent like Marco Balich, who honors our country across the world, and I hope that our paths will cross again in the future. I think I understood what his secret is while reading an interview he gave some time ago: "A man is moved when he allows himself to be amazed as a child does. When they ask me if I still have a child in me, I always say yes, very much so: I always think bigger."

Alessandro Del Piero

FIRE AND ICE

Opera Meets Pop at the Arena di Verona

If the origins of ice skating date back to more than one thousand years ago in Sweden, we have Pieter Bruegel the Elder to thank for one of the most beautiful paintings depicting skaters in action, *Winter Landscape with Skaters and a Bird Trap*, from 1565.

The idea of building a story around the world of figure skating, of representing the ancient struggle between good and evil, love and hate, fire and ice, resulted in a spectacular performance in one of the most revered symbols of opera, the Arena di Verona. The show combined the talent of some of the world's best skaters with the tradition of a musical genre that captivates a passionate audience all over the world.

The opening scene, featuring a violin player towering over the stage on top of an iceberg, introduced, in a crescendo of piercing sounds, a frozen world in which men and women fight against each other, with no possibility of communication. Love, in a vortex of passion and sensuality, is the force that can spark the fire capable of melting the ice: obscurity and isolation finally succumb to the strength of pure feeling. The fire that was stolen from the gods by Prometheus was reinterpreted here in a more modern fashion, with dance and music making a lasting emotional impression on the audience witnessing an amazing sporting and musical virtuosity, its strength and beauty telling a classic story of opposites confronting each other.

Thanks to the power of love, unifying and energizing, a verdant nature blossomed from the ice, initiating a sensuous spring that led to a final joyful celebration.

The athletes' performance complemented the artistic elements of a show combining sporting talent with classical music and pop tunes. Skaters moved on the stage fluidly and with determination; the amazing suppleness of their bodies and their artistic talent were a demonstration of a skilfulness that was freed from all rules, with the sole aim of representing a show of great power and enchanting beauty.

"Pure joy"

Taking part in such a unique show, in such an exceptional location as the Arena di Verona, was a great honor for me. It was an even greater honor, and pure joy, to have the opportunity to play a central role in this wonderful achievement, together with incredibly talented Italian and international athletes.

I felt huge admiration, and I still do when I think back to those days, for the orchestra, the choir, the singers, the dancers, and the whole production, who contributed to a magical atmosphere that we were able to share with an enthusiastic audience.

I hope to have the chance to relive those emotions again with Marco, and to work once more with so many extraordinary champions and artists.

Carolina Kostner

When a man is
tired of London,
he is tired of life
Season of mists and
mellow fruitfulness
The Walrus and
The Carpenter

SEE YOU IN RIO!

London 2012 Olympic and Paralympic Flag Handover

During the Olympic and Paralympic ceremonies, the flag handover is constituted by a solemn formal moment, the passing of the Olympic or Paralympic flag from the host city to the one where the next edition of the Games will take place, followed by a representation of the mood of the ceremonies to come.

After the flag handover in Salt Lake City in 2002, which announced the Torino 2006 Olympics, the ceremonies presented here took place during the London 2012 Games, giving a glimpse of what to expect from Rio de Janeiro, Brazil, in 2016.

For the Olympic closing ceremony, the choice was to tell an unusual and ethically progressive story: a street cleaner teaching the values of the *carioca* samba, the definitive Brazilian dance, to a man in an official uniform – very far from the idea of "party" that connotes Brazil all over the world.

The scenery and costumes did the rest, with music accompanying the rhythmic movements of a fascinating machine representing Yemanjá, the goddess of water: a very important element in a country like Brazil, which possesses some of the largest water reservoirs in the world, such as the majestic Amazon River.

The ceremony continued with the entrance of a group of dancers who paid tribute to the country's indigenous heritage, evoking the spirits of the forest with their rhythmic dance and chanting, but at the same time hinting at the inherent modernity of the indigenous sustainable lifestyle with a high-tech reinterpretation of traditional costumes. This performance was followed by other examples of the rich musical and ritual culture of Brazil: from the Maracatu dancers, characters linked to the history of plantations in the Northeast of the country, to Capoeira, the martial art and dance style created by the slaves coming from the African continent. In the show's finale the legendary Edson Arantes do Nascimiento, better known as Pelé, the greatest footballer in Brazil, and perhaps in the whole planet, entered the scene, while a giant reproduction of the Rio Games logo alluded to the figurative embrace that Brazil offers to the world.

The second flag handover, represented during the closing ceremony of the Paralympics, dealt with the theme of disability by expressing the value of a shared experience between able and disabled people, understood as human beings that are not that different from each other, and are entitled to the same prospects and happiness. This flag handover went to the heart of the problem, dismissing stale conventions.

A joyful celebration of Brazil's melting pot of cultural influences allowed able and disabled performers to experience together the harmony of dance, the beauty of the body's movements and the pleasure of unconditional sharing. With a central, crucial message: no discrimination should be tolerated by a truly evolved society.

TO BE, OR
NOT TO BE
That is the question

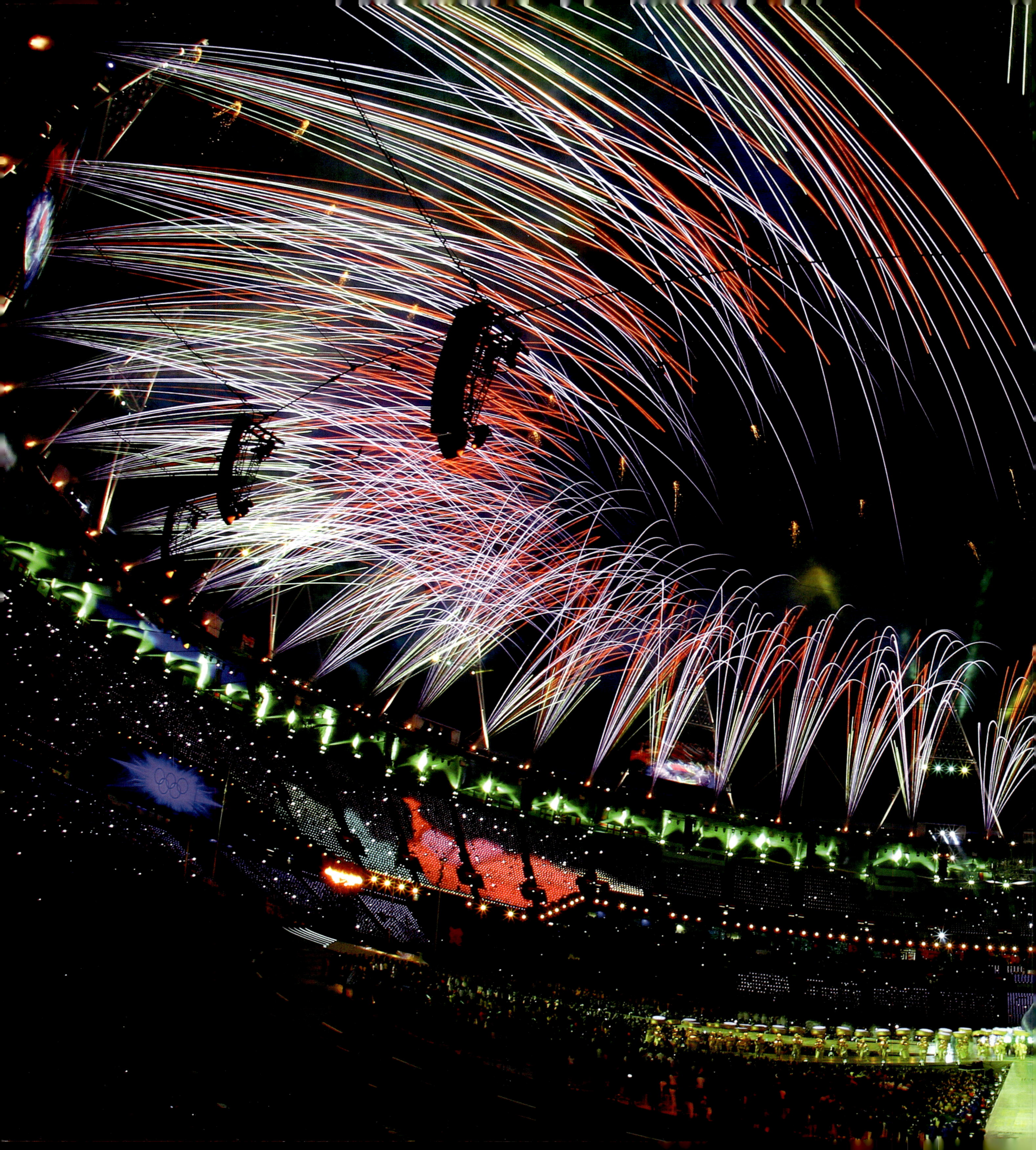

A New Vision of the World:
A Conversation with
Marco Balich

Moreno Gentili: How would you describe your work?

Marco Balich: *I create shows with the aim of amazing the people—big and complex productions, from Olympic ceremonies to national celebrations, from official openings to live spectacles.*

M.G.: What objectives do you pursue with your creative language?

M.B.: *The objective is to convey emotions that are simple and easily understandable in a spectacular way, with very cultural and conceptual references. I think it is necessary to know how to talk to all cultures with a universal creative language, to deliver clear and grand statements in a manner that makes them truly unforgettable. This is a skill possessed by few talented people, who are capable of mastering different creative media (such as music, literature, visual arts, and design) to express an effective message to millions of people with different cultural and geographical backgrounds.*

M.G.: What are the creative and research premises necessary to tackle an experience of this magnitude?

M.B.: *To approach an Olympic ceremony or a large-scale international event you must study hard to acquire an in-depth knowledge of a country, its cultural and sporting traditions, its different histories,* and to involve the best local talents for the best possible delivery.

M.G.: How do you deal with the responsibility of your role?

M.B.: *The beauty of working for events of this scale lies in the fact that such ceremonies always coincide with a moment of great joy for a country, a region, a city. The aim for my team and I is to awaken and inspire pride in the people of the host country, who are showcasing themselves to the rest of the world.*
The responsibility of this role requires a serious approach and a deep emotional involvement. The ceremonies we create are great achievements from any point of view, and great statements that explore global themes.
It is important to avoid cynicism, and to trust humankind as the fundamental and central element in the development of the universe. We believe in the highest values of humanity and we respect them.

M.G.: What are your sources of inspiration?

M.B.: *In order to put together a solid conceptual foundation for the stories we want to tell, we seek inspiration from a combination of various elements, first of all a curiosity for the world and its diverse cultures, which I share with a great creative team.*

We draw our inspiration mainly from the people. What stimulates us creatively is contemporary art, street theater, big youth gatherings, music events of all genres, niche performances, sophisticated theater plays, opera, great rock concerts, beautiful books, photographs, even traditions and sayings.
All this is obviously reinterpreted through the lens of our Italian DNA, for which design and beauty are always present as a framework and as an essential element of our mise-en-scène: the structure of our shows has to be pure and complex at the same time.

M.G.: On the subject of your team, is this your secret? Would you like to tell us something about the outstanding people in it?

M.B.: *I work with a core group of people who I feel a deep connection with, and who have been with me for many years. It is a group of exceptional talents who together have reached worldwide recognition by delivering outstanding shows: Gianmaria Serra, Simone Merico, Annalisa Barbieri, Lulu Helbaeck, Simona Rivetta, Laura Caopelli, Claudia Cattai, and Gloria Cerù; without them I would not have achieved all the unforgettable moments that are shown in this book.*
To these I should add a series of figures with whom we have had the honor of collaborating for a long time. I will mention Doug Jack Bryn Walters and Nikos Lagousakos, great choreographers; Christophe Berthonneau, the king of pyrotechnics; Daniele Finzi Pasca, a fantastic director; and Marco Astarita, skillful production manager.
We have the privilege of working with the best professionals from all over the word, and this sharing of so many different experiences is what makes our ceremonies rather unique on the international event scene. For this we consider ourselves to be very lucky.

M.G.: Who are the people who have inspired you most?

M.B.: *I have been especially inspired by four people: Mark Fisher, who has been the greatest stage and set designer for live shows in the world, and has worked with the likes of U2 and Pink Floyd, as well as on the Torino and Beijing Olympics and many Cirque du Soleil productions. Then Lida Castelli, who is fundamental for the fantastic visual impact of the shows I have designed and has been by my side in my creative development since the 2002 flag handover in Salt Lake City. Stefano Coffa, a visionary partner and a great human being. And finally Ric Birch, who has taught me a lot, sharing his experience from unforgettable Olympic ceremonies such as Los Angeles in 1984, Barcelona in 1992, and Sydney in 2000.*

M.G.: How do you choose your experts and what do you ask them?

M.B.: *When we assemble a creative group we build a very diverse team, specifically suited to deliver a unique show. The secret in this job is to look always for fresh energy and outstanding individuals who feel the urge to make big statements. It is crucial that every person we involve is ready to be part of a very ambitious, open, hard-working, multicultural, respectful, and unprejudiced team.*

M.G.: You are involved in the Rio 2016 Olympics. Can you tell us something about this?

M.B.: *Brazilians embrace you, welcome you and seduce you with their stunning landscapes, fabulous music and a very simple and easy lifestyle. We are letting ourselves be inspired by these values, absorbing an in-depth knowledge of this culture.*

M.G.: Since the first Olympics of the modern era were organized in 1896, taking part in them has always been a dream for every athlete. You managed to do so in a completely different way, creating immensely

captivating emotions for the audience. What was it like to have such a close encounter with the Olympics?

M.B.: *The Olympics are the most important recurrent event of the planet, and therefore an Olympic ceremony is the mother of all shows. They embody the highest level of show business, of technology, of ceremonial pomp, of responsibility on a global level. Approaching the Olympics is an honor, a pleasure, a challenge, and a great endeavour, loaded with expectations.*

M.G.: Sport ceremonies today also carry a universal message of peace. Why?

M.B.: *The world of large-scale events and celebrations was effectively born in the 1980s, with the opening ceremonies of Moscow 1980 and Los Angeles 1984, which were followed in Europe by the Barcelona 1992 Olympics. Since then, these types of shows have become colossal statements that all countries in the world compete to produce.*
The origin of these ceremonies dates back to the first modern Olympics of 1896 in the Athens stadium, with the exceptional vision of Baron de Coubertin, and developed into the games of Berlin 1936, which the brutal genius of Albert Speer celebrated with an unforgettable ceremony created by Leni Riefenstahl. Today we fortunately celebrate humanity and pay tribute to different values such as world peace, the respect of competition, and equality through sport.
The Olympics possess a unifying force stronger than the United Nations, as the whole planet feels a connection with the Olympic rings. This has meant that, over the course of time, the ceremonies of the Games have grown around a very strict protocol; attending these ceremonies has become the highest aspiration for athletes around the world, and an unequaled peak in global TV audiences, with a presence of heads of state in numbers far superior to any other sporting or

political event around the globe. It is for this reason that these shows can have an unrivaled influence in shaping values and raising profiles.

M.G.: When creating Olympic and Paralympic ceremonies, how do you deal with the theme of disability, especially in terms of "ethical communication" to the world?

M.B:. For me the Olympics and the Paralympics have the same value. I really object to handling disability in a different way. I believe that Paralympic athletes are equal to able-bodied ones, or actually even stronger. I love courage, people who challenge rules, who break the mold, and those who tear down barriers like the Paralympic athletes do, and as such are worthy of our admiration as much as the hundred-meter runner who breaks the nine-second barrier.
I make no distinctions between people with or without disabilities, men, women, people with different sexual orientations, of any skin color or religious belief; for me every person is essentially a human being and must be treated with respect.

M.G.: Having established that creativity is crucial to bring your projects to life, how important is technology in the creation of your events?

M.B.: *Technology is fundamental in the world of events, but it is always at the service of creativity: we should never let ourselves be seduced by a great technological innovation that today appears to be extraordinary but will shortly become obsolete and rather dull. We definitely need technology, but it is only a tool and not an objective.*

M.G.: You have a past in the production of big music events. What is left of this in your memory?

M.B.: *The attraction and the adrenaline of a live*

music event were clear to me since my childhood, after having seen Paul McCartney in Venice's San Marco square in 1974, a concert in which the first lasers were used. The sense of deep emotion, which only an event connecting thousands of people at the same time can deliver, is a wonderful feeling that transcends age and geography.

My career began precisely with the organization of concerts, which was a great formative experience in terms of learning about the essential elements of a production; I then went on to work on more creative endeavors, starting from music videos, and going on to big television productions and live events. From there I reached what I consider to be the highest expression of the live show industry worldwide, the Olympic ceremony. The adrenaline that kicks in when you feel the attention of millions of people is unique.

Working on big concerts, but also on music videos, has taught me to multitask, to manage any possible and unpredictable situation linked to the specific needs of an event. What you learn is that at a given time—generally at 8:00 p.m. for live concerts, and at 7:00 a.m. for film sets—you have to make sure that a combination of elements is ready and set in motion simultaneously.

I apply this on a larger scale to the Olympics: I make sure that many different activities developed over the course of three years converge toward the countdown of the opening ceremony.

M.G.: Does being Italian influence your style?

M.B.: *Being born in Venice, and growing up in a country that has given so much to the world in terms of culture, history, and art, is an absolute privilege. I see this as an added value for our ceremonies, in which great attention is paid to beauty; for this reason our shows and events are considered to be rather different from the work of our competitors.*

I am a proud Italian who loves his country, but I see myself as a citizen of the world: I appreciate my roots as much as I love people from all countries, all ethnic groups, all genders, all backgrounds. I am a great fan of humanism and a supporter of the Renaissance concept of man at the center of the universe.

M.G.: We still recall the "red skaters" from the Torino 2006 Olympics, one of your events that is famous to this day for its creative innovation and the quality of its visual inventiveness.

What are the most beautiful moments that you remember from your work, or the ones you feel a deeper emotional connection with?

M.B.: *Plenty of beautiful moments come to mind. Aside from the one you mention, I would say the surge of emotion in Turin when the Dove of Peace was revealed. Or the "Grito," the collective cheer at the end of the Mexico Bicentennial, or the time when we gathered under the Abruzzi skies thousands of people who could still feel the echoes of the earthquake and yet generously took part in the Mediterranean Games. I think back to a wonderful and windy evening at -15° (Celsius) on the roof of the stadium in Salt Lake City in 2002, when we saw the projections for our flag handover segment for the first time on the ice of the field of play. I remember how we reimagined, staging it in a sensational way, the Flight of the Angel during the Venice Carnival, with Handel's "Hallelujah" booming and one hundred thousand people looking up.*

During exhausting travels I go back to those memories, and to cheer myself up I read blogs and comments on social media from all those who have been touched by our work. In those moments I understand the value of what we do, and how we are able to give people a sense of joy and belonging. This is the greatest motivation that accompanies me across the world.

M.G.: What are the values you would you like to pass on to young people?

M.B.: I am aware that we are luxury nomads who produce hugely expensive ceremonies around the world, but we still have the moral duty to inspire young people, to inject hope into the new generations, and also to influence them in their ethics and conduct. I give you an example: Our ceremonies enlist the support of thousands of volunteers, who participate for free and with absolute generosity. Volunteers represent an important element of our ceremonies, and for this reason we make sure that the whole structure works on the basis of kindness and respect, regardless of one's place in the show's hierarchy. This is a great lesson for young people and for everyone, including us, on how relations between different roles should function in a hierarchical structure.

I have had the chance to work on some of the most exciting projects in the world, with the best artists and professionals on the international scene—I think I have been very lucky, but I have also pushed myself to seize every opportunity that brought me closer to my objective. If I had to give one piece of advice to young people, it would be this: be brave, be passionate, and follow your vision.

Marco Balich

Biography

Marco Balich is referred to as the "designer of emotions."

His long journey in the field of entertainment began in the music world, organizing concerts for international stars; his artistic path successfully led him to explore music videos, television, and any creative territory involving emotion, sound, and vision.

By partnering with Filmmaster Group, for over 20 years, Marco Balich progressively established his worldwide reputation. From 2002 to 2013, the Event division, under his guidance, successfully produced a wide variety of large scale shows reaching international recognition: from Olympic ceremonies to stadium openings, to international sporting events, festivals and celebrations.

Some of his most acclaimed shows are the launch of the new Fiat 5C0 (Turin, Italy, 2007), the opening of the Donbass Arena (Donetsk, Ukraine, 2009), the Mexico 2010 Bicentennial celebrations, the opening of the Juventus Stadium (Turin, Italy, 2011), and Intimissimi on ice OPERAPOP (Arena di Verona, Italy, 2014). Marco Balich is one of the world's leading Olympic ceremony creators, (the Salt Lake City 2002 Flag Handover; Torino 2006 Olympic and Paralympic ceremonies; London 2012 Olympic and Paralympic Flag Handover ceremonies; and Sochi 2014 Olympic closing ceremony and Paralympic ceremonies) his work has been reworded, in 2006, with an Emmy award.

He is also the Executive Producer of the 2016 Olympic ceremonies in Rio de Janeiro and the Artistic Director of the Padiglione Italia (Italian Pavilion) - Expo 2015, Milan. Together with Simone Merico and Gianmaria Serra, he founded, Balich Worldwide Shows, a visionary company based in Milan that creates, develops, and produces large-scale events, Olympic ceremonies, permanent shows and new ground breaking formats.

ACKNOWLEDGMENTS

This book would not have been possible
without the contribution of

Special thanks to
Gianmaria Serra, my longtime teammate and dear friend
Lida Castelli, the best artistic director I have worked with
Simone Merico, a smiling dreamer
The IOC and Patrick Stalder for their kind cooperation
All the volunteers, without whom no ceremony could be made

Thanks to the team of Balich Worldwide Shows
Lara Bortoluzzi, Laura Cappelli, Claudia Cattai, Gloria Cerù, Silvia Guenzi, Lulu Helbaek, Francesca Martinazzo,
Claudio Perosa, Simona Rivetta

Filippo Baracchi, Annalisa Barbieri, Elena Castorina, Fulvio Cesaroni, Maria Chiara Corelli, Olivia Esteri, Simone Ferrari,
Gennaro Emiliano Girasole, Julian Hill, Doug Jack, Paola Jussi, Giuditta Lombardi, Sara Maestro, Lisa Misaylidi,
Stefania Opipari, Maia Pedrotti, Francesca Robbiati, Alessandra Rossetti, Paolo Scaglia, Michele Telaro, Valentina Valverde

Thanks to my family
Anita, Lola, Pilar and Zeno, Francesca, Aurelio and Brenda, Laura and Lisa

Thanks to

Bina and Pramod Agarwal, Andrea Agnelli, Rinat Akhmetov, Marco Albano, Luca Alberti, Maria Grazia Alfisi, Alfredo Accatino, Isabel Allende, Anghela Alò, Claudia Alongi, Carola Altissimo, Giuseppe Arena, Giorgio Armani, Alberto Artese, Marco Astarita, Simona Atzori, M k Auckland, Fabrizio Audagnotto, Silvia Aymonino, Massimo Babini, Vanessa Barreiro, Silvia Battaglio, Ivars Beitans, Serena Belladelli, Mauro Belloni, Riccardo Benini, Paolo Berruti, Miriam Bertaina, Christophe Berthonneau, Sara Berutto, Valeria Bigioggera, Ric Birch, Marco Boarino, Florian Boje, Tiberio Boido, Emanuela Bolle, Roberto Bolle, Giampiero Boniperti, Angelo Bonissoni, Maria Bonzanigo, Daniele Borin, Giovanna Boschetti, Caterina Botticelli, Patrice Bouqueniaux, Diana Bracco, Marco Broll, Carla Bruni, Adam Burke, Catherine Buyse, Giovanna Buzzi, Eugenio Caballero, Massimo Cacciari, Leonardo Caetaro, Antonio Calbi, Valeria Campo, Giancarlo Campora, Marina Cappelli, Giacomo Carissimi, Elio Carmi, Alberto Carmignani, Valentino Castellani, Francesco Cattani, Tomaso Cavanna, Geo Cavazzano, Juri Ceccotti, Michele Centonze, Juri Chechi, Catharina Chen, Dmitry Chernyshenko, Lorenzo Cherubini, Alexey Chuvashev, Nathan Clarke, Stefano Coffa, Valentina Colarusso, Coolio, Enzo Cosimi, Sir Philip Craven, Enrico Cremonesi, Giovanni Criscione, Joseph Cristiani, Debbie Cronshaw, Daniele Cuffaro, Michael Curry, Fabrizio D'Oria, Lino Dainese, Daniela Dal Cin, Manuel Dall'Olio, Roberto Daneo, Kate Dawkins, Vittorio De Amicis, Luca De Meo, Marianne de Wit, Alessandro Del Piero, Stefano Del Piero, Es Devlin, Mario Di Marco, Sue Dhaliwal, Christophe Dubi, Nick Eltis, Konstantin Ernst, Franco Faggiotto, Massimo Faggiotto, Alexander Faifman, Andrea Faini, Paola Fantato, Nicola Ferrari, Alice Ferraro, Daniele Finzi Pasca, Mark Fisher, Guido Foa, Ferruccio Forcella, Joe Frisina, Saverio Frittella, Alejandra Gadea, Hugo Gargiulo, Glenda Genovesi, Lorenzo Gentile, Irene Gerini, Beatrice Giannini, Michael Gill, Silvia Giorgi, Scott Givens, Abel Gomes, Xavier Gonzalez, Michela Gottardello, Fabrizia Greppi, Phil Green, Leonardo Gryner, Maria Guleghina, Laura Guglielmetto, Cao Hamburger, Julie Hamelin, Richard Hartman, Phil Hayes, Matt Higgins, Sam Hunter, Sumant Jayakrishnan, Milla Jovovich, Martin Kallen, Firat Kasapoglu, Maria Kazachkova, Christina King, Konstantin Kirkarian, Nobuhiko Kiyohara, Carolina Kostner, Dimitra Kritikidi, Nikos Lagousakos, Andreas Lakner, Stéphane Lambiel, James Lee, Alfonsina Lettieri, Evgeniya Levchitskaya, Sidney Levy, Ric Lipson, Sophia Loren, Jean-Michel Louis, Mauricio García Lozano, Roberto Lun, Marco Maccapani, Flavio Machado, Eneas Mackintosh, Diego Maggi, Giulia Mancini, Monica Manganelli, Sigrid Mangilli, Nicoletta Mantovani, Ivan Manzoni, Francesca Marchi, Durham Marenghi, Adriano Martella, Gina Chan Martinez, Giovanni Masera, Renata Melo, Fernando Meirelles, Reinhold Messner, Ritika and Rohan Metha, Lourdes Milano, Alessandra Miori, Angela Missoni, Margherita Missoni, Marisa Monte, Riccardo Monti, Francesca Montinaro, Marie-France Montine, Alessandra Montresor, Valentina Moretti, Bill Morris, Pierre Mussche, Simona Muti, Karla Nagel, Jum Nakao, Tiziana Nasi, Andrey Nasonovskiy, Nadia Nasonovskaya, Francisco Negrin, Carlos Arthur Nuzman, Anna Offelli, Matteo Oioli, Alessio Olivieri, Yoko Ono, Triinu Onton, Giorgio Orlandini, Sergey Palkin, Jimmy Pallas, Daniele Palmieri, Paola Panzeri, Emanuela Papone, Antonio Parente, Luca Parisse, Julien Pateau, Sam Pattinson, Laura Pausini, Fabio Pavanetto, Luciano Pavarotti, Michael Payne, Gerolamo Pellicanò, Giovanni Perosino, Andrea Peruffo, Davide Pesce, Gabriella Pescucci, Luc Petit, Cristiana Picco, Michel Platini, Irina Prokhorova, Paolo Quarino, Chandra Ramirez, Patrizia Rastelli, Mónica Raya, Gianvito Riccio, Marina Roberti, Jacques Rogge, Paola Rossetto, Giulio Rovelli, Aroldo Ruschioni, Emanuela Sabbatino, Romain Sabella, Stratos Safioleas, Olivia Salvadori, Matteo Salvi, Alessandro Sandiano, Kenrick Sandy, Sara Santini, Susan Sarandon, Paola Schlaepfer, Bruno Schnebelin, Daniela Selloni, Piers Shepperd, Elena Shubina, Rocky Smith, Stjin Snaet, Franca Sozzani, Giulia Staccioli, Christel Strohn, Matteo Tagliabue, Nicola Tallino, Nicola Tamburrano, Roberto Tarasco, Claire Terri, Daniela Thomas, Pierre-Yves Toulot, Cesare Vaciago, Gabriele Vacis, Jorge Vargas, Andrea Varnier, Celina Padilla Vázquez, Koert Vermeulen, Sandro Veronesi, Renata Vieitas, Andrucha Waddington, Bryn Walters, Ray Winkler, Patrick Woodroffe, Julia Whittle, Susana Yamauchi, Alberto Zambernardi, Alex Zanardi, Juan Carlos Canfiels Zapata

America's Cup Events Authority, Commonwealth Games Federation, FC Shakhtar Donetsk, FIAT, International Committee of Mediterranean Games, International Olympic Committee, International Paralympic Committee, Italian Navy, Juventus Football Club, Municipality of Venice, Rio 2016 Olympic Games Organising Committee, Union of European Football Associations

CREDITS

Cover: Juventus Stadium Opening. Turin, Italy 2011. Photo by Luca Parisse
pp. 4-5: Torino 2006 Olympic Games, Closing Ceremony. Turin, Italy 2006. Photo by Thierry Nava
pp. 6-7: Sochi 2014 Paralympic Games, Opening Ceremony. Sochi, Russia 2014. Photo by Luca Parisse
pp. 8-9: Intimissimi on ice OPERAPOP. Arena di Verona, Verona, Italy 2014. Photo by Luca Parisse
pp. 10-11: Sochi 2014 Olympic Games, Closing Ceremony. Sochi, Russia 2014. Photo by Luca Parisse
pp. 12-13: México 2010 Bicentennial of Independence. Mexico City, Mexico 2010. Photo by Stratos Safioleas
pp. 14-15: FC Shakhtar Donetsk 75th Anniversary. Donetsk, Ukraine 2011. Photo by Luca Parisse
pp. 16-17: Orascom Pyramids Project. Giza, Egypt 2007. Photo by Nick Jones courtesy of Durham Marenghi
pp. 18-19: Juventus Stadium Opening. Turin, Italy 2011. Photo by Luca Parisse
pp. 20-21: London 2012 Olympic Games, Rio 2016 Flag Handover Ceremony. London, UK 2012. Photo by Luca Parisse
pp. 22-23: Delhi 2010 Commonwealth Games, Aerostat Project. Delhi, India. Photo by Joan Lyman / M&M Production Management
pp. 24-25: Festa del Redentore. Venice, Italy 2009. Photo by Christoph Maier
p. 26: "Love" Venice New Year's Eve. Venice, Italy 2008. Photo by Massimo Vitali
p. 29: Torino 2006 Olympic Games, Closing Ceremony. Turin, Italy 2006. Photo by Giorgio Sottile
pp. 32-33: Sochi 2014 Paralympic Games, Closing Ceremony. Sochi, Russia 2014. Photo by Luca Parisse
p. 36: Sochi 2014 Paralympic Games, Closing Ceremony. Sochi, Russia 2014. Photo by Luca Parisse
pp. 38-39: Sochi 2014 Olympic Games, Closing Ceremony. Sochi, Russia 2014. Photo by Luca Parisse
p. 40: Sochi 2014 Paralympic Games, Opening Ceremony. Sochi, Russia 2014. Photo by Luca Parisse
p. 41: Sochi 2014 Paralympic Games, Opening Ceremony. Sochi, Russia 2014. Photo by Luca Parisse
pp. 42-43: Sochi 2014 Olympic Games, Closing Ceremony. Sochi, Russia 2014. Photo by Luca Parisse
p. 44: Sochi 2014 Paralympic Games, Opening Ceremony. Sochi, Russia 2014. Photo by Luca Parisse
p. 45: Sochi 2014 Paralympic Games, Opening Ceremony. Sochi, Russia 2014. Photo by Luca Parisse
pp. 46-47: Sochi 2014 Paralympic Games, Closing Ceremony. Sochi, Russia 2014. Photo by Danil Kolodin
pp. 48-49: Sochi 2014 Olympic Games, Closing Ceremony. Sochi, Russia 2014. Photo by Luca Parisse
pp. 50-51: Sochi 2014 Paralympic Games, Opening Ceremony. Sochi, Russia 2014. Photo by Luca Parisse
pp. 52-53: Sochi 2014 Olympic Games, Closing Ceremony. Sochi, Russia 2014. Photo by Luca Parisse
pp. 54-55: Sochi 2014 Paralympic Games, Closing Ceremony. Sochi, Russia 2014. Photo by Luca Parisse
p. 56: Sochi 2014 Paralympic Games, Closing Ceremony. Sochi, Russia 2014. Photo by Danil Kolodin
p. 57: Sochi 2014 Paralympic Games, Closing Ceremony. Sochi, Russia 2014. Photo by Danil Kolodin
pp. 58-59: Sochi 2014 Paralympic Games, Closing Ceremony. Sochi, Russia 2014. Photo by Luca Parisse
pp. 60-61: Sochi 2014 Paralympic Games, Closing Ceremony. Sochi, Russia 2014. Photo by Luca Parisse
pp. 63: Yoko Ono, Copyright © 2006, Used by permission, all rights reserved
p. 64: México 2010 Bicentennial of Independence. Mexico City, Mexico 2010. Photo by Adam Wiseman
pp. 66-67: México 2010 Bicentennial of Independence. Mexico City, Mexico 2010. Photo by Ariette Armella
pp. 68-69: México 2010 Bicentennial of Independence. Mexico City, Mexico 2010. Photo by Shawna Tavsky
pp. 70-71: México 2010 Bicentennial of Independence. Mexico City, Mexico 2010. Photo by Shawna Tavsky
p. 72: México 2010 Bicentennial of Independence. Mexico City, Mexico 2010. Photo by Stratos Safioleas
p. 73: México 2010 Bicentennial of Independence. Mexico City, Mexico 2010. Photo by Adam Wiseman
pp. 74-75: México 2010 Bicentennial of Independence. Mexico City, Mexico 2010. Photo by Shawna Tavsky
pp. 76-77: México 2010 Bicentennial of Independence. Mexico City, Mexico 2010. Photo by Shawna Tavsky
pp. 78-79: México 2010 Bicentennial of Independence. Mexico City, Mexico 2010. Photo by Omar Franco Pérez Reyes / Corbis
p. 82: Napoli 2012 America's Cup World Series. Naples, Italy 2012. Photo by Rosario Facciolla
pp. 84-85: Napoli 2012 America's Cup World Series. Naples, Italy 2012. Photo by Rosario Facciolla
p. 86: Napoli 2012 America's Cup World Series. Naples, Italy 2012. Photo by Rosario Facciolla
p. 87: Napoli 2012 America's Cup World Series. Naples, Italy 2012. Photo by Saverio Scattarelli
pp. 88-89: Napoli 2012 America's Cup World Series. Naples, Italy 2012. Photo by Rosario Facciolla
pp. 90-91: Napoli 2012 America's Cup World Series. Naples, Italy 2012. Photo by Rosario Facciolla
p. 94: New Fiat 500 World Premiere. Turin, Italy 2007. Photo by Giorgio Sottile
p. 96: New Fiat 500 World Premiere. Turin, Italy 2007. Photo by Giorgio Sottile
p. 97: New Fiat 500 World Premiere. Turin, Italy 2007. Photo by Giorgio Sottile

p. 98: New Fiat 500 World Premiere. Turin, Italy 2007. Photo by Giorgio Sottile
p. 99: New Fiat 500 World Premiere. Turin, Italy 2007. Photo by Giorgio Sottile
pp. 100-101: New Fiat 500 World Premiere. Turin, Italy 2007. Photo by Giorgio Sottile
p. 102: New Fiat 500 World Premiere. Turin, Italy 2007. Photo by Giorgio Sottile
p. 103: New Fiat 500 World Premiere. Turin, Italy 2007. Photo by Giorgio Sottile
pp. 104-105: New Fiat 500 World Premiere. Turin, Italy 2007. Photo by Giorgio Sottile
pp. 106-107: New Fiat 500 World Premiere. Turin, Italy 2007. Photo by Giorgio Sottile
pp. 108-109: New Fiat 500 World Premiere. Turin, Italy 2007. Photo by Giorgio Sottile
p. 112: "Sensation" Venice Carnival. Venice, Italy 2008. Photo by Rodrigo Molina/Unionpress for Vela S.p.A.
pp. 114-115: Festa del Redentore. Venice, Italy 2009. Photo by Alessandro Belgiojoso
pp. 116-117: "Sensation" Venice Carnival. Venice, Italy 2009. Photo by Marco Parente/Unionpress for Vela S.p.A.
pp. 118-119: Festa del Redentore. Venice, Italy 2009. Photo by Christoph Maier
p. 120: "Sensation" Venice Carnival. Venice, Italy 2008
p. 121: "Love" Venice New Year's Eve. Venice, Italy 2009. Photo by Marco Parente/Unionpress for Vela S.p.A.
p. 122: "Sensation" Venice Carnival. Venice, Italy 2009. Photo by Nicola Ferrari
p. 123: "Sensation" Venice Carnival. Venice, Italy 2008
pp. 124-125: Festa del Redentore. Venice, Italy 2009. Photo by Alessandro Belgiojoso
pp. 126-127: Festa del Redentore. Venice, Italy 2008. Photo by Rodrigo Molina/Unionpress for Vela S.p.A.
p. 130: Love Forever: A Fairy Tale Wedding. Puglia, Italy 2014. Photo by Luca Parisse
pp. 132-133: Love Forever: A Fairy Tale Wedding. Puglia, Italy 2014. Photo by Luca Parisse
p. 134: Love Forever: A Fairy Tale Wedding. Puglia, Italy 2014. Photo by Luca Parisse
p. 135: Love Forever: A Fairy Tale Wedding. Puglia, Italy 2014. Photo by Paola Cominetta
pp. 136-137: Love Forever: A Fairy Tale Wedding. Puglia, Italy 2014. Photo by Luca Parisse
pp. 138-139: Love Forever: A Fairy Tale Wedding. Puglia, Italy 2014. Photo by Luca Parisse
pp. 140-141: Love Forever: A Fairy Tale Wedding. Puglia, Italy 2014. Photo by Luca Parisse
p. 142: Love Forever: A Fairy Tale Wedding. Puglia, Italy 2014. Photo by Paola Cominetta
p. 143: Love Forever: A Fairy Tale Wedding. Puglia, Italy 2014. Photo by Paola Cominetta
pp. 144-145: Love Forever: A Fairy Tale Wedding. Puglia, Italy 2014. Photo by Luca Parisse
p. 146: Love Forever: A Fairy Tale Wedding. Puglia, Italy 2014. Photo by Luca Parisse
p. 147: Love Forever: A Fairy Tale Wedding. Puglia, Italy 2014. Photo by Luca Parisse
pp. 148-149: Love Forever: A Fairy Tale Wedding. Puglia, Italy 2014. Photo by Paola Cominetta
p. 152: Torino 2006 Olympic Games, Opening Ceremony. Turin, Italy 2006. Photo by Vladimir Rys/Getty Images
pp. 154-155: Torino 2006 Olympic Games, Opening Ceremony. Turin, Italy 2006. Photo by Pool/Getty Images
p. 156: Torino 2006 Olympic Games, Opening Ceremony. Turin, Italy 2006
p. 157: Torino 2006 Olympic Games, Opening Ceremony. Turin, Italy 2006. Photo by Vladimir Rys/Getty Images
pp. 158-159: Torino 2006 Olympic Games, Opening Ceremony. Turin, Italy 2006. Photo by Kevork Djansezian/Getty Images
p. 160: Torino 2006 Olympic Games, Closing Ceremony. Turin, Italy 2006. Photo by Giorgio Sottile
p. 161: Torino 2006 Olympic Winter Games, Opening Ceremony. Turin, Italy 2006. Photo by Kevork Djansezian/Getty Images
p. 162: Torino 2006 Olympic Games, Opening Ceremony. Turin, Italy 2006. Photo by Matt Dunham/Corbis
p. 163: Torino 2006 Olympic Games, Opening Ceremony. Turin, Italy 2006. Photo by Clive Rose/Corbis
pp. 164-165: Torino 2006 Olympic Games, Opening Ceremony. Turin, Italy 2006. Photo by Giorgio Sottile
p. 166: Torino 2006 Olympic Games, Opening Ceremony. Turin, Italy 2006. Photo by Daniel Dal Zennaro /Corbis
p. 167: Torino 2006 Olympic Games, Opening Ceremony. Turin, Italy 2006. Photo by Sampics /Corbis
pp. 168-169: Torino 2006 Olympic Games, Closing Ceremony. Turin, Italy 2006. Photo by Giorgio Sottile
p. 170: Torino 2006 Paralympic Games, Opening Ceremony. Turin, Italy 2006. Photo by Roberto Borgo
p. 171: Torino 2006 Paralympic Games, Opening Ceremony. Turin, Italy 2006. Photo by Roberto Borgo
pp. 172-173: Torino 2006 Olympic Games, Opening Ceremony. Turin, Italy 2006. Photo by Thierry Nava
p. 175: Isabel Allende, *Tales of Passion*, TED2007
p. 176: Donbass Arena Opening Ceremony. Donetsk, Ukraine 2009. Photo by Shakhtar FC
pp. 178-179: Donbass Arena Opening Ceremony. Donetsk, Ukraine 2009. Photo by Shakhtar FC
pp. 180-181: Donbass Arena Opening Ceremony. Donetsk, Ukraine 2009. Photo by Shakhtar FC
p. 182: Donbass Arena Opening Ceremony. Donetsk, Ukraine 2009. Photo by Shakhtar FC
p. 183: Donbass Arena Opening Ceremony. Donetsk, Ukraine 2009. Photo by Shakhtar FC

pp. 184-185: FC Shakhtar Donetsk 75th Anniversary. Donetsk, Ukraine 2011. Photo by Luca Parisse
pp. 186-187: FC Shakhtar Donetsk 75th Anniversary. Donetsk, Ukraine 2011. Photo by Luca Parisse
p. 188: FC Shakhtar Donetsk 75th Anniversary. Donetsk, Ukraine 2011. Photo by Luca Parisse
p. 189: FC Shakhtar Donetsk 75th Anniversary. Donetsk, Ukraine 2011. Photo by Luca Parisse
pp. 190-191: FC Shakhtar Donetsk 75th Anniversary. Donetsk, Ukraine 2011. Photo by Luca Parisse
pp. 192-193: FC Shakhtar Donetsk 75th Anniversary. Donetsk, Ukraine 2011. Photo by Luca Parisse
pp. 194-195: Donbass Arena Opening Ceremony. Donetsk, Ukraine 2009. Photo by Shakhtar FC
p. 196: UEFA Euro 2012 Opening Ceremony. Warsaw, Poland 2012. Photo by Luca Parisse
pp. 198-199: UEFA Euro 2012 Opening Ceremony. Warsaw, Poland 2012. Photo by Luca Parisse
pp. 200-201: UEFA Euro 2012 Opening Ceremony. Warsaw, Poland 2012. Photo by Luca Parisse
p. 202: UEFA Euro 2012 Opening Ceremony. Warsaw, Poland 2012. Photo by Shaun Botterill/Getty Images
p. 203: UEFA Euro 2012 Opening Ceremony. Warsaw, Poland 2012. Photo by Bartolomiej Zborowski /Corbis
pp. 204-205: UEFA Euro 2012 Opening Ceremony. Warsaw, Poland 2012. Photo by Luca Parisse
p. 206: UEFA Euro 2012 Closing Ceremony. Kiev, Ukraine 2012. Photo by Luca Parisse
p. 207: UEFA Euro 2012 Closing Ceremony. Kiev, Ukraine 2012. Photo by Luca Parisse
pp. 208-209: UEFA Euro 2012 Closing Ceremony. Kiev, Ukraine 2012. Photo by Luca Parisse
pp. 210-211: UEFA Euro 2012 Closing Ceremony. Kiev, Ukraine 2012. Photo by Luca Parisse
p. 214: Pescara 2009 Mediterranean Games, Opening Ceremony. Pescara, Italy 2009. Photo by Luca Parisse
pp. 216-217: Pescara 2009 Mediterranean Games, Opening Ceremony. Pescara, Italy 2009. Photo by Luca Parisse
p. 218: Pescara 2009 Mediterranean Games, Opening Ceremony. Pescara, Italy 2009. Photo by Luca Parisse
p. 219: Pescara 2009 Mediterranean Games, Opening Ceremony. Pescara, Italy 2009. Photo by Stringer/Getty Images
pp. 220-221: Pescara 2009 Mediterranean Games, Opening Ceremony. Pescara, Italy 2009. Photo by Stringer/Getty Images
pp. 222-223: Pescara 2009 Mediterranean Games Opening Ceremony. Pescara, Italy 2009. Photo by Stringer/Getty Images
p. 226: Juventus Stadium Opening. Turin, Italy 2011. Photo by Luca Parisse
pp. 228-229: Juventus Stadium Opening. Turin, Italy 2011. Photo by Luca Parisse
pp. 230-231: Juventus Stadium Opening. Turin, Italy 2011. Photo by Luca Parisse
p. 232: Juventus Stadium Opening. Turin, Italy 2011. Photo by Luca Parisse
p. 233: Juventus Stadium Opening. Turin, Italy 2011. Photo by Luca Parisse
pp. 234-235: Juventus Stadium Opening. Turin, Italy 2011. Photo by Luca Parisse
pp. 236-237: Juventus Stadium Opening. Turin, Italy 2011. Photo by Luca Parisse
pp. 238-239: Juventus Stadium Opening. Turin, Italy 2011. Photo by Luca Parisse
p. 242: Intimissimi on ice OPERAPOP, Arena di Verona, Verona, Italy 2014 . Photo by Luca Parisse
pp. 244-245: Intimissimi on ice OPERAPOP. Arena di Verona, Verona, Italy 2014. Photo by Luca Parisse
pp. 246-247: Intimissimi on ice OPERAPOP. Arena di Verona, Verona, Italy 2014. Photo by Paola Cominetta
p. 248: Intimissimi on ice OPERAPOP. Arena di Verona, Verona, Italy 2014. Photo by Paola Cominetta
p. 249: Intimissimi on ice OPERAPOP. Arena di Verona, Verona, Italy 2014. Photo by Paola Cominetta
pp. 250-251: Intimissimi on ice OPERAPOP. Arena di Verona, Verona, Italy 2014. Photo by Paola Cominetta
p. 252: Intimissimi on ice OPERAPOP. Arena di Verona, Verona, Italy 2014. Photo by Paola Cominetta
p. 253: Intimissimi on ice OPERAPOP. Arena di Verona, Verona, Italy 2014. Photo by Paola Cominetta
pp. 254-255: Intimissimi on ice OPERAPOP. Arena di Verona, Verona, Italy 2014. Photo by Luca Parisse
pp. 256-257: Intimissimi on ice OPERAPOP. Arena di Verona, Verona, Italy 2014. Photo by Paola Cominetta
p. 260: London 2012 Olympic Games, Rio 2016 Flag Handover Ceremony. London, UK 2012. Photo by Luca Parisse
p. 262: London 2012 Olympic Games, Rio 2016 Flag Handover Ceremony. London, UK 2012. Photo by Luca Parisse
p.263: London 2012 Olympic Games, Rio 2016 Flag Handover Ceremony. London, UK 2012. Photo by Hannah Peters/Getty Images
pp. 264-265: London 2012 Olympic Closing Ceremony Flag Handover. Photo by Luca Parisse
p. 266: London 2012 Paralympic Games, Rio 2016 Flag Handover Ceremony. London, UK 2012. Photo by Luca Parisse
p. 267: London 2012 Paralympic Games, Rio 2016 Flag Handover Ceremony. London, UK 2012. Photo by Luca Parisse
p.268-269: London 2012 Olympic Games, Rio 2016 Flag Handover Ceremony. London, UK 2012. Photo by Paul Gilham/Getty Images
p. 270: Salt Lake City 2002 Olympic Games, Torino 2006 Flag Handover Ceremony. Salt Lake City, USA 2002. Photo by Jacques Demarthon/Getty Images
p. 273: Sochi 2014 Paralympic Games, Closing Ceremony. Sochi, Russia 2014. Photo by Luca Parisse
p. 276: Love Forever: A Fairy Tale Wedding. Puglia, Italy 2014. Photo by Paola Cominetta
p. 278: "Sensation" Venice Carnival. Venice, Italy 2009. Photo by Luca Ghidoni/Getty Images

Salt Lake City 2002 Olympic Games, Torino 2006 Flag Handover Ceremony. Salt Lake City, USA 2002
produced by Linkage

Torino 2006 Olympic Games, Opening and Closing Ceremonies. Turin, Italy 2006
Torino 2006 Paralympic Winter Games, Opening Ceremony. Turin, Italy 2006
produced by K2006

New Fiat 500 World Premiere. Turin, Italy 2007
Orascom Pyramids Project. Giza, Egypt 2007
Pescara 2009 Mediterranean Games, Opening Ceremony. Pescara, Italy
Donbass Arena Opening Ceremony. Donetsk, Ukraine 2009
Delhi 2010 Commonwealth Games, Aerostat project. Delhi, India
produced by K-Events

"Love" Venice New Year's Eve. Venice, Italy 2008-2009
"Sensation" Venice Carnival. Venice, Italy 2008-2010
Festa del Redentore. Venice, Italy 2008-2009
produced by Venezia Marketing & Eventi

México 2010 Bicentennial of Independence. Mexico City, Mexico
produced by Instantia Producciones

FC Shakhtar Donetsk 75th Anniversary. Donetsk, Ukraine 2011
Juventus Stadium Opening. Turin, Italy 2011
Napoli 2012 America's Cup World Series Opening. Naples, Italy 2012
UEFA Euro 2012 Opening Ceremony. Warsaw, Poland 2012
UEFA Euro 2012 Closing Ceremony. Kiev, Ukraine 2012
produced by Filmmaster Events

London 2012 Olympic Games, Rio 2016 Flag Handover Ceremony. London, UK 2012
London 2012 Paralympic Games, Rio 2016 Flag Handover Ceremony. London, UK 2012
produced by CC2016

Sochi 2014 Olympic Games, Closing Ceremony. Sochi, Russia 2014
Sochi 2014 Paralympic Games, Opening and Closing Ceremonies. Sochi, Russia 2014
produced by Balich Worldwide Shows and CSA

Love Forever: A Fairy Tale Wedding. Puglia, Italy 2014
produced by Balich Worldwide Shows

Intimissimi on ice OPERAPOP. Arena di Verona, Verona, Italy 2014
produced by Balich Worldwide Shows, Intimissimi, Opera on ice

BIOGRAPHIES

Lida Castelli

Lida Castelli has been working alongside Marco Balich as artistic director on all his events.
She was communications director for Italian designer Moschino for ten years, coediting with him the book *X Anni di Kaos!,* and subsequently worked for fashion brand Prada.
She was artistic director for the flag handover at the Olympic closing ceremony of Salt Lake City 2002, art director supervisor for the opening and closing ceremonies of the Torino 2006 Olympic Games and of the opening ceremony of the Paralympic Games of the same year. From 2008 to 2010 she was artistic director of Venice's New Year's Eve, Carnival and Festa del Redentore.
In 2012 she was the artistic director of the UEFA Euro 2012 opening and closing ceremonies in Poland and Ukraine, and artistic consultant for the Rio 2016 flag handover ceremonies during the London 2012 Olympic Games.
In 2014 she directed the Sochi Paralympic closing ceremony. She is artistic consultant for the Rio 2016 Olympic ceremonies.

Moreno Gentili

Moreno Gentili is a content strategist, as well as a fiction and theater writer.
Some of his books are *Viaggi di Memoria*, Bompiani; *La Ferrari*, Skira; *Milano 1944, un amore*, Skira; *In Linea d'Aria*, Feltrinelli; *Sguardo Nomade*, Archinto; *L'Inferno Dentro*, Sonda; *On the Move*, Skira; *Suite Sarajevo*, Archivi del '900; *African Heroes*, Skira.
He is the author of several projects for Italian and international companies, such as the design for the Guzzini Museum in Recanati; the new Formula 1 boxes for Ferrari; *On the Move* for Autogrill with Al Gore, Steven Spielberg, Marc Augé and other authors to tell the story and achievements of the company in the world; *Harmonia Mundi*, a permanent display for the new Rcs and *Corriere della Sera* headquarters in Milan; *Vulcania*, a permanent installation for the new Fiat Centro Stile in Turin; *Skira Impresa*, publishing project aimed at representing Italian design and production in the world.
As an artist focused on the concept of sustainability he took part in the 2007 Venice Biennial at Fondazione Thetis with the project *Do Not Cross*, designed to promote the protection of European forests, and exhibited a work devoted to New York at the 2011 Venice Biennial.

Balich Spectacular Shows

Art Direction
Lida Castelli

Texts by
Moreno Gentili

Graphic Design and Layout
Stefano Frattini

Translation by
Sara Maestro

Editorial Coordination
Sara Maestro
Lidia Rossi

Production
Sergio Daniotti

First published in the United States of America in 2015
by Rizzoli International Publications, Inc.
300 Park Avenue South
New York, NY 10010
www.rizzoliusa.com

Originally published in Italy in 2015 by
RCS Libri S.p.A.
© 2015 RCS Libri S.p.A., Milan

The publisher would be pleased to hear from rightholders of any unidentified
iconographic sources.

2015 2016 2017 2018 / 10 9 8 7 6 5 4 3 2 1

ISBN: 978-0-8478-4671-9

Library of Congress Control Number: 2015932103
Printed in Italy

www.balichws.com

Printed in March 2015
by EBS - Verona, Italy